Cradle Crew

Royal Canadian Air Force
World War II

D1121328

Kenneth K. Blyth

Cradle Crew

Royal Canadian Air Force World War II

by Kenneth K. Blyth

Sunflower University Press®

1531 Yuma • P. O. Box 1009 • Manhattan, Kansas 66505-1009 USA

© 1997 by Kenneth K. Blyth
Printed in the United States of America on acid-free paper.

Cover design, Jeffrey E. Blyth

ISBN 0-89745-217-8

Edited by Ruth Ann Warren

Layout by Lori L. Daniel

THE BOMBERS

Whenever I see them ride on high
Gleaming and proud in the morning sky
Or lying awake in bed at night
I hear them pass on their outward flight
I feel the mass of metal and guns
Delicate instruments, deadweight tons
Awkward, slow, bomb racks full
Straining away from the downward pull
Straining away from home and base
And I try to see the pilot's face
I imagine a boy who has just left school
On whose quick-learnt skill and courage cool
Depend the lives of the men in his crew
And success of the job they have to do
And something happens to me inside
That is deeper than grief, greater than pride
And though there is nothing I can say
I always look up as they go their way
And care and pray for everyone,
And steel my heart to say,
            "Thy will be done".

                                        Sarah Churchill

This book is dedicated to:

My wife Sarah and my family, Jeff,
Susan, Nancy, Carol, and Deborah,
who would not be here today if I had
made a minor rudder adjustment
at the time of the attack;

and to the dedicated members of the Cradle Crew:

Jim Taylor — Navigator
Darrell "Atky" Atkinson — Bombardier — in memoriam
Douglas Grey — Engineer
Adam "Wat" Watson — Wireless Air Gunner
Brock Folkersen — Mid Upper Gunner — in memoriam
Ray "Curly" Hughes — Tail Gunner

Contents

Acknowledgments

"The Bombers" — Sarah Churchill, reprinted with permission from The Lady Soames, Sarah Churchill's Literary Executor.

Spencer Dunmore and William Carter. *Reap the Whirlwind*. Canada: Crécy Books, Ltd., 1992.

> The only specific information I used came from Appendix B, pages 392-393. This dealt with the number of aircraft in the individual raids in which I participated and the number of losses. Other information in the book validated what I already remembered about the sorties in which I participated.

Hubert Zemke. *Zemke's Stalag*. Washington, D.C.: Smithsonian Institution Press, 1991.

> Because Zemke became the Allied camp commandant while I was in Sta-

lag Luft 1, his book provided the factual names of some of the German officers. I was there at that time, and I participated in some of the incidents he describes.

Murray Peden. *A Thousand Shall Fall*. North York, Ontario: The Stoddart Publishing Company, Ltd., 1992.

> I have used Peden's analogy of what it was like to fly a bomber on a night mission. Reprinted with permission.

Manifred Boehme. *Jagdgeschwader 7: Die Chronik eines ME-262-Geschwaders 1944-45*. Stuttgart, 1983. Reprinted with permission.

> Dr. Ottmer, of Militargeschichtliches Forschungsamt, has provided me with several pages in German of Manifred Boehme's book describing the German recollection of the events of March 31, 1945. I have had this transcribed into English and have used it to develop my Foreword. I have endeavored to write this Foreword in the same style as the balance of my book.

James M. Taylor, the navigator in our crew, researched the library and correlated the newspaper headlines with each of our missions.

Jeffrey E. Blyth assisted in an editorial capacity during the preparation of this work.

Foreword

*F*OR THE PAST 50 years I have regaled my family and friends with many of the stories in this book. They have enjoyed the wartime personal experiences of the Cradle Crew that flew the Handley Page Halifax bombers with the Royal Canadian Air Force during World War II. My close friends, Cal and Bill Ollerhead, have encouraged me to document those experiences, part of the nostalgia half a century after the Big War: training experiences, raids over enemy targets, being shot down over Germany, life in a prison camp, and finally release at war's end by the Russians.

The author, Flying Officer Kenneth K. Blyth — taken at graduation as a Pilot Officer, Saskatoon, Saskatchewan, Canada, December 10, 1943.

Fear, like pain, thankfully is forgotten in time. The reader may feel that I have treated our fears in a cavalier manner, but it was not my intention to do so. To my mind, none of these exploits were heroic — they were simply the experiences of seven very young men serving their country with no thought of reward, yet at the same time placing their lives on the line each time they took off on a mission.

I have tried to describe these experiences as I did to my children, and as I would if I were talking to you; and while this style may not be the formal literary style usually found in such a manuscript, I believe if I were to do otherwise, the story would lose some of the personal touch I am trying to capture.

It is quite possible these adventures will stir up similar, almost forgotten memories of your own. Should they do so, write down your memories, or tell them to your good friends; but most importantly, tell them to your children. This book, then, will have accomplished what I set out to do.

Flying Officer Kenneth K. Blyth

Prologue

*T*HE YEAR WAS 1939 and life was easy. The Great Depression was behind us. King George VI and Queen Elizabeth had visited Canada in June and had dedicated the World War I monument in Ottawa, Canada's capital, then proceeded across Canada on a good-will tour. War clouds were forming in Europe, but no one was paying too much attention.

The Capital City Boys Band was excited. They were competing in the National Band Competition at the Canadian National Exhibition in Toronto, Ontario. Captain Finlayson, the director,

The Cradle Crew alongside *E.Q.-Johnny*: Ken Blyth — pilot, Jim Taylor — navigator, Darrell "Atky" Atkinson — bombardier, Adam "Wat" Watson — wireless operator, Doug "Pop" Grey — engineer, Brock Folkersen — mid-upper gunner, and Ray "Curly" Hughes — tail gunner, January 1945.

had been there on two previous occasions with this same band, receiving two first-place prizes. On the second occasion he had also taken a junior band, which received second-place recognition. He, too, was anxious to compete again. The captain had received his appointment during World War I and had continued to teach music as a career in the Ottawa school system. He was a tough taskmaster. Though often seeming to be deaf when in conversation, when it came to music he could turn his back on the ensemble while we were rehearsing, then swing around and walk up to one of the musicians and say, "You are playing a *B* natural instead of a *B* flat."

We had practiced long and hard for almost a month in latter July and August and could perform the test piece, "The Wanderer," at what he thought was a competitive level. We traveled by bus from Ottawa to Toronto. The competition was held in an open band shell. The judges' tent stood in front of the band shell, facing away, so that they could hear the bands' presentations but could not see them. When the order of presentation was decided by lot, we drew fourth out of some twelve contestants. Each band was allowed one "warm-up number" before the test piece. Captain Finlayson always used a hymn, because it allowed him to evaluate the tone quality of the band. He told us later that the judges always knew that it was his band — we were the only ones playing a hymn.

Our band had at least 40 musicians, with a good balance of brass, reed, and percussion. I must confess that at the time I was a mediocre clarinet player. One of our major competitors was the Montreal all-brass band, which used a coronet for the solo work usually given to a reed instrument. This was their signature of sorts to the judges. They had competed before, and we felt sure the judges recognized this group as well, without being told when they were performing.

When the judges came out and said, "The band that played fourth is the winner of the competition," we were amazed! Captain Finlayson was overjoyed that we were once more a success. His age would preclude him from ever again bringing a group to this competition.

The next morning, September 1, we awoke to the headline "GERMANS BOMB POLAND." Within 30 days Poland would be completely taken over by the Germans and Russians. On September 3, 1939, every newspaper in Canada put out an extra edition, and newsboys ran through the streets shouting, "Get your extra! Read all about it! Great Britain declares war on Germany!"

World War II had started. But at 16 we were not too interested; we were more impressed with our win at the competition.

Three years later that would change.

The logo on the nose of *E.Q.-Johnny*.

Introduction

LL WAS QUIET AT *Jagdgeschwader 7 in the early hours of the morning on March 31, 1945. No enemy flights had been reported, and everyone was fast asleep. For the previous two weeks the Strahler Fighter Squadron's JG-7 had been intoxicated by the impressive number of air victories they had achieved. They needed the extra rest.*

Suddenly an alarm rang and everyone rushed to his appointed station. Everything happened so fast that Flieger Gerhard Reiher pulled on his flight suit over his pajamas. Apparently

The Cradle Crew — taken in Manchester, England, early 1945. Atky, Ray, Jim, and Doug; Wat, Ken, and Brock.

English and Canadian bombers had slipped in from the West under the radar screens, using confusing directional changes, and had finally approached their German destinations: Wilhelmshaven, Bremen, and Hamburg. The Strahler Fighter Squadron, made up of four jet fighter units of Messerschmitt ME-262s, did not know it at that time, but this was to be a day of air battle victories that would never be surpassed.

The first group of ten planes, under the command of Oberleutnant Stehle, lifted off at 8:05 a.m. The fighter tracking station at Stade, some 23 miles due west of Hamburg, guided this fighter unit to a pack of 40 Lancasters in the area over Bremen. The Allied bombing stream was well protected by its own fighters, and the German attackers were only able to inflict minimal damage.

At 8:15 a.m., as soon as Stehle's group was airborne, a second group of ME-262s took off under the command of 28-year-old Oberleutnant Hans Grunberg, who proudly wore the Ritterkreuztrager (Knight's Cross, a decoration higher than the Iron Cross). The ground installations directed Grunberg's group to one of the bomber waves that had already reached the port area of Hamburg. The eight aircraft in Grunberg's formation approached the city some 1,000 meters above the bombing stream.

Because the Allies' intended target was under cloud cover, their dark-painted bombers stood out dramatically. In the words of one of the ME-262 pilots, "they looked like bedbugs crawling on a sheet." The German pilots looked down on the Lancaster and Halifax deployments and saw they were without fighter support. And for a daylight raid, the gaggle formation was unusually dispersed. The usual daylight raid found the gaggle tightly grouped, and German fighters would have to look for potential targets of opportunity at the outside of the gaggle.

This was no neophyte fighter unit. Grunberg had flown some 500 sorties with 77 aerial victories; Franz Schall, 525 sorties with 117 aerial victories; Gustav Sturm, 130 sorties and 16 victories; Hans Todt, 50 sorties and 11 aerial victories; and Gerhard Reiher and Friedrich Wilhelm Schenk, 1 aerial victory apiece.

Grunberg shouted "Nichts wie draufk!" — "Attack, Attack!" and the strike began. Apparently the Allied bombers had not expected such extensive resistance. A direct hit by one of the fighters completely destroyed a Lancaster. Gerhard Reiher hit one or two more Lancasters, without paying attention to whether they burned or crashed. The bombers tried to escape the ME-262s with corkscrew maneuvering, to no avail. The fighters followed them with their twisting actions. The effect of the 50mm R4M salvos rockets and 30mm MK 108 cannons was devastating. The site was an air massacre! Fighters could see twirling aluminum shreds, dismantled wings with spinning engines, ripped open fuselages, exploding fuel tanks, and dozens of parachutes. The end of the fighting came only when the fighters' fuel and ammunition were exhausted.

It was really unimportant whether the hits were confirmed or not. The end of the war was at hand, and this was pure self-gratification.

The remains of the bombing stream were already limping home when one lone Halifax appeared and made its bombing run. Three of the pilots from JG-7 spotted the straggler, and Oberleutnants Hans Grunberg and Franz Schall together with Flieger Gerhard Reiher turned to make one last attack. They moved in above and behind the bomber, and their leader, Grunberg, fired a shot that knocked out the guns in the tail turret and hit the port outer wing, setting it on fire. No need to worry about this one, thought Grunberg; it would not be bombing any more German targets. *E.Q.-Queenie*, on fire and out of control, started spinning toward the clouds below.

JG-7 claimed 13 air victories without a single loss.

Later that same day, Stehle, with the forces under his command, added to the victories, claiming six more successes when they attacked a stream of Lancasters supporting an American air offensive near Osnabrück. The day was a disaster for the Allied air forces. Out of 489 bombers participating in the raid on Hamburg, 200 were from the Canadian Six Group. The Canadians experienced the loss of 8 bombers, the most since the attack on Hamburg on July 28-29, 1944, when 22 were lost.

Fortunately for the Allies, the number of German ME-262s in operation at this point in the war was minimal; otherwise, it is conceivable that air losses could have been even greater.

Chapter 1

German Hospitality

"*A*NYONE HERE FROM *South Saskatchewan?*"

Being questioned about South Saskatchewan is not unusual if you happen to live in Western Canada; but it is somewhat strange when the question is asked by a German prison guard at the entrance to Stalag Luft 1, where a group of Canadian and American aircrew prisoners of war were being introduced to the new way of life they would be subjected to for the next several months.

The date was April 5, 1945.

In this somewhat homogenous group of American, Australian,

British, and Canadian aircrew prisoners, there were 30 of us, some of whom had been captured a few weeks earlier. We had spent the better part of a week in Dulag Luft Centers but were now being placed in permanent internment facilities until the end of the war.

We were a scruffy lot — unshaven, unbathed, discouraged, disappointed, and some even relieved — unlike those inside the gate who were reasonably well clothed and clean shaven and who had come to greet the new arrivals, and to see if there was anyone they knew in the group.

Once inside the gate, we looked at our surroundings, while behind us one of the guards slammed the gate shut and made sure it was securely locked. All the huts inside the compound were plain, rectangular buildings, most of which were used for housing the POWs. We were led to one that apparently served as an administrative headquarters.

We, too, hoped we would see at least one familiar face — a face that everyone at our individual bases had given up for lost. No such luck. None of our group appeared to know any of those immediately greeting us. Inside the compound everyone seemed reasonably content and busy — doing we knew not what, but somehow busy.

As part of the documenting process, we had to disrobe in order for the Germans to catalogue what few possessions we still had on our person. They would find very little on the Canadian and British aircrews, for we had been instructed to carry nothing with us that the Germans might be able to use in their interrogations. We all still wore whatever clothing or uniform we had had on when we were captured. The first order of business for the Germans was to take away all government-issue effects, such as watches or pens, and if necessary outfit us in prison garb.

Underneath my battle dress flying uniform I wore a chamois vest that was primarily for warmth, because the aircraft at high altitudes was bitter cold. My mother had sent it to me from Canada. Each time before setting off on a mission over Germany I would outline a bomb on the vest in ink. When I returned from each mission I would fill in the outline of the bomb with my pen. Eighteen bombs were completely filled in, and there was the outline of the 19th.

I had completed two more missions than my crew. So that I would not be a total neophyte when I took my own on its first mission, it was required that I fly as "second dickie" (copilot) with two experienced crews on actual raids on enemy targets. I do not know where the term "second dickie" came from. I had no official function with their crew. You might say I just went along as a passenger — possibly a valuable passenger in an emergency, but for the present I was excess baggage.

One of the guards, noticing the vest with the bomb markings, asked me in English, "Planes shot down?"

Having gone through intensive interrogation earlier without the threat of a firing squad, we were getting a little cocky. We felt that the life-threatening period was over, so I answered "Yes." A look of amazement crossed his face and the faces of the other guards who could understand English. They thought they had shot down a fighter pilot, not knowing I flew a bomber.

Jim Taylor, my navigator, and Darrell Atkinson, bombardier, had similar vests. Watching this reaction by the guards, they decided to follow my lead. Their vests had 16 completed bomb markings and the outline of a 17th. When they opened their battle dress jackets and unveiled them they did so in a slower, more deliberate and dramatic manner. The eyes of the guards really popped when they saw this additional evidence of German aircraft shot down. The guards must have believed they had blown three Allied fighter aces out of the sky. They looked at one another and held an

Stalag Luft 1, Barth, Pomerania.

animated conversation; we would have given anything to know just what was said.

We were then led to a large shed containing delousing equipment. Our clothes were placed in an oven heated to extremely high temperatures. Not only did this process remove any lice, it shrank our chamois vests and a fleece-lined flying jacket of one of the American fliers to a size that could possibly have fit a Barbie doll.

After the delousing, we were provided with our first American Red Cross parcel, the first of many that would be given to us like clockwork every week that we were in the camp.

One of the resident Kriegies (pronounced "kreegees") met us and divided our group among the other prisoners in several huts. ("Krieg Gefangenen" — or "Kriegies" for short — was the German word for prisoner of war. The full name was a mouthful, and we all became just plain "Kriegies.") Atky, Jim, and I, all officers, were in one hut, and my four NCOs — Wat, Doug, Ray, and Brock — were in another. We had our first POW meal, one of the amazing repasts that could be produced from our Red Cross parcels, together with the small quantities of food we received from our captors. Under the Geneva Convention we were supposed to be fed the same food that was eaten by the German military. The Red Cross parcels were an add-on. At the Dulag Center we had one meal before being placed in our cells; it was the same menu fed to guards at the next table. To say it was frugal was putting it mildly. German prisoners in Canada and the United States, by comparison, lived in the lap of luxury.

Room 11, Hut 13, was to be our home. That first night we slept on the floor. We were finally able to take a shower, and it felt great — we had not removed our clothing for the previous six days. All of us were exhausted and were soon fast asleep.

Our camp, Stalag Luft 1, was the very first German prisoner of war camp of World War II. Located on the Baltic Sea just outside the town of Barth in Pomerania, some 60 miles almost due west of Berlin, it was considered a small camp, with only 9,000 prisoners.

Stalag Luft 1 had opened in 1940 for captured Royal Air Force personnel. It was in a remote location with a high water table, which made escape by tunneling difficult. The following year it had two compounds — one for officers (an Olag) and the other for the other ranks (a Stalag). The correct name for the camp was Kriegsfangenerlager No. 1 der Luftwaffe, shortened to Stalag Luft 1. At the outset, and for some time, it was an officers-only camp. North 1, 2, and 3 were subsequently added, but the original west compound remained the primary unit because it was near the Vorlager, the front part of the camp outside the barbed-wire compound, which contained the German administration buildings, the hospital, workshops, and stores. The west compound had about 1,400 U.S. and 890 British and Allied POWs. The other compounds contained almost entirely American prisoners. West had latrine buildings — but they were actually outhouses that had to be emptied weekly by the Germans. I was surprised they did not have us assigned to such duties. Later on we had to do that for health reasons.

Chapter 2

Enlistment

BACK IN OTTAWA, in the spring of 1942, Ken Simpson, a close buddy of mine, and I had talked about joining the armed services. What undoubtedly contributed to this was watching the movie **Captains of the Clouds**, starring James Cagney and Dennis Morgan, being filmed in Ottawa. We were both 18, and we were impressed by the movie and anxious to do our part in the war effort. Besides, our jobs had become a little boring compared to the excitement of being in the Armed Forces. We decided to wait until fall and join the Royal Canadian Air Force.

The mere thought of her oldest son enlisting was a traumatic experience for my mother, a widow of eight years. During World War I my father had been a machine gunner in the trenches when the Germans started using mustard gas. The gas had caused my father's heart to become enlarged. After the war he tried to get a soldier's pension, but it took him until 1933 to succeed. At that time they gave him five years to live. He died from a stroke 13 months later. He had four brothers, and all but one enlisted in World War I. My uncle Ken, after whom I am named, returned from the war with a quarter of a lung and died shortly thereafter. None of the five are alive today.

My mother had her own personal recollections of the first war. Her brother Harry, living in Quebec City, Quebec, invited her to leave her home in Oldham, England, and to live in Canada. Her other brothers had all been killed in the war, and with her father's death she was alone. Her trip on the SS *Esperian* was a nightmare. Just off the coast of Ireland the boat was torpedoed by a German submarine, and she spent a sleepless night in a lifeboat where nearly everyone was seasick before being rescued the following day. She lost her few remaining possessions. Fortunately, a friend convinced her that she should take the next boat to Canada. She did, and this time the trip across the Atlantic was uneventful.

Shortly after leaving high school I started a small dance band, Jump and Jive with Kenny Blyth. During those early war years we would play twice a week at the Red Triangle Club in Ottawa. On the other nights, servicemen who regularly played in the military and Air Force bands provided the entertainment. It was a busman's holiday for them. Douglas Deane, an Australian, ran the facility, which catered to thousands of servicemen. Many of the major firms in the city, such as the Metropolitan Life Insurance Company, provided hostesses, and we enjoyed playing to the servicemen and their partners. Indirectly, seeing so many young Canadians in uniform undoubtedly contributed to my joining when I became old enough to do so.

On the evening of October 25, 1942, Ken Simpson and I went down to the recruitment depot. Because Ken wore glasses, he was not accepted, but they gave me a rating of A1B A3B, which apparently was what was required medically to be accepted. I now had to await the call for posting to a Manning Depot.

Seventeen days later, November 11, 1942, I arrived at #5 Manning Depot, Lachine, just outside Montreal, Quebec. I was alone in a mass of hopeful aircrew candidates, eager to be outfitted in the uniform of the

Royal Canadian Air Force. Regardless of how important the recruits thought they might have been in civilian life, for the next indefinite period they would be known as "Acey Deuceys" or Aircraftsmen Second Class. No one in the RCAF held a lower rank.

Although I made many new friends at the Manning Depot, the one that I recall most vividly was Bruce Motley, from Hamilton, Ontario. It sounded as if everyone in his hometown knew him. He said he had tried out for the Hamilton Tiger-Cats, a Big Four Football team. After the war I developed considerable business for the Chesapeake & Ohio Railway Company in the Hamilton area, but to this day I have never come across a single soul that has ever heard of him. He was a great guy, and on one of our weekend leaves I took him home with me. I told him my mother would undoubtedly prepare my favorite dinner, a deep-dish meat pie with a golden crust, the whole works poured over mashed potatoes. I let him know my mother would be disappointed if he didn't ask for seconds. He played it safe and asked for thirds. My mother, unaware of my admonition to Bruce, wanted to know where I had found him and if the RCAF fed us at all. I never saw Bruce again after Manning Depot. Maybe he never returned from overseas.

Life at the Manning Depot was a strange experience for all of us, and it took some time getting used to. Manning Depots were the pride and joy of corporals and sergeants. The officers reveled in bossing around the new recruits. I have to admit we moved when they shouted commands. They used their patented gags every day with questions like, "Is there anyone here who would like to be a pilot?"

Hands would shoot up, and after selecting one or two of the volunteers, the corporal would say, "I would like you to pilot these brooms around the biffy and hop to it."

We didn't seem to learn their routine, for a day or so later the same corporal would ask, "Anyone here planning to be a navigator?" Once again the hands would shoot up. We had bit on it again. "You would-be navigators can navigate these paint brushes up and down the outside of the mess hall. Get a move on!" And so it went.

Everyone took his turn at "KP" — kitchen patrol — and the only good thing we could say about that assignment was that we ate well. Many of the assignments were simple ones like dishing out oatmeal or turning the spigot on the milk container. But it was work when we had to do this some 2,000 times at the meal hour.

While we spent some of the day in elementary classes on the Air Force, a good part of the day was spent in drill parade. Finally we were given aptitude tests to determine whether or not we were candidates for aircrew. Many were disappointed; some would end up as ground crew if they remained in the active Air Force. My educational background was limited to high school, and I had problems with some of the math questions. It looked like my dream of being a pilot was going up in smoke, and I was stressed out waiting to get the result. My concerns were valid, because I had not done well. Fortunately, I was able to convince the testing officer that if they would enroll me in the WETP — War Emergency Training Program — course I felt sure I could meet the aircrew standards. He said, "Blyth, if you weren't so damn keen on this I would turn you down, but I am going to recommend that you attend WETP."

Not intending to be flippant, I answered, "Keane by name and keen by nature." (My middle name is Keane, my mother's maiden name.)

WETP, or as we called it, "the Wet P course," meant three months living in boarding houses in downtown Montreal with the other class members and attending classes in mathematics, physics, and English at the University of Montreal. It was a great experience. Frankly, we were being paid for having a good time.

Our per diem for living out was reasonable, but not nearly enough as far as we were concerned. We spent most of our evenings at a mansion on Sherbrooke Street called Lady Davis' House. This was a great place to get low-cost meals, and Lady Davis had organized young ladies' groups to act as hostesses. They had to commit to two nights a week, and although they were not to get involved with the Air Force types, it was impossible for them not to, to some degree. Lady Davis would receive invitations from many of the well-to-do families in Montreal for servicemen to come to dinner, and we jumped at the opportunity to have some home cooking. Only noncommissioned personnel were permitted in the Lady Davis' House, so all the servicemen could relax and have a great time.

We were given quite a number of weekend passes from the university, and my buddies from Ottawa and I would take the train home. It was about this time that we started calling one another by our initials. I was "KK," and a new friend, Fred Davey, was "TF." He was quite a character. His luggage for the weekend was a toothbrush. His favorite pastime was trying to cheat the train conductor out of his fare. A railroad conductor would start from each end of the train collecting fares and working in toward the center. If the train reached a small town before the conductors got to TF, he would jump off and run around one or the other of the conductors, then climb back on board. He kept a supply of used ticket stubs that he would put on his seat should they come back to recheck. Most of the time he got away with it.

On one particular trip the train was delayed and the conductors were closing in on TF. It looked like he was trapped and would have to pay his fare. No way. The railcar was an old sleeper coach, so he opened the bunk above his seat, climbed in, closed it partially, and left it open a crack for air. But when the conductor opened the door, it caused the bunk door to close on TF. It looked liked he would have to call for help. Not Fred. He was going to stick it out. Unfortunately, an old lady had a question or two to ask the conductor, and by the time the conductor had left our coach and we pulled TF out of the upper bunk he was just about asphyxiated. That was the last time he tried that one.

TF remained with me for quite a bit of my training, and he was always trying to get away with something. His clothes were never pressed, he shaved only when he had to, and he would turn his shirt inside out rather than have it laundered. He epitomized P. O. Prune, whom I will tell you about in a later chapter. TF's parents were such refined people it was difficult to imagine why he followed such a routine.

I have to say the three months went by quickly, and soon it was time for our final exams. Most of the class passed easily. Fun time was over; we were now ready to get down to business and start actual training.

Chapter 3

Bowls Out for Barley

*T*HE MAJORITY OF THE PRISONERS in Stalag Luft 1
were Americans.

The Germans recognized Colonel Hubert Zemke, the
senior-ranking American officer, and acknowledged him
as the ranking POW officer in the camp. Colonel Zemke had
been shot down while flying a P-47 Thunderbolt sometime during November 1944.

Equivalent in rank, Group Captain Cecil Weir was the senior
officer of the British, Australian, and Canadian forces in the
camp. They appeared to work very well together.

The Germans had many POW camps sprinkled throughout Germany, most of which were placed near military installations or potential bombing targets. The Germans reasoned that the Allies would not bomb targets where there was a possibility of a misplaced bomb landing in a POW camp. Stalag Luft 1 was in an open area, within a quarter of a mile of the Baltic Sea, and other than the town of Barth, there was nothing of any consequence for miles. The location concept must have been developed sometime after Stalag Luft 1 was built.

Barth was a typical small German town whose inhabitants — while undoubtedly curious about the prison camp on the outskirts of their community — never let their curiosity cloud their better judgment; they stayed clear of the installation. And we were somewhat oblivious to the fact that there was a town nearby.

Our camp was divided into many sections to make it extremely difficult for prisoners to formulate or carry out escape plans. We were not permitted to go from one section to another. Although I have been unable to validate it, the story was that only one prisoner escaped from Stalag Luft 1, in spite of the fact that some 90 attempts had been made. The one escapee managed to get 36 miles from Barth before he was recaptured and returned to solitary confinement in the camp.

At the time of our capture we had been placed in a Dulag Luft Interrogation Center, where we had been imprisoned in individual cells. We were unprepared for the POW quarters at Stalag Luft 1. My first impression was that the camp was not unlike our Manning Depot accommodations. That is, it had a parade square, surrounded by small buildings that housed us. This is where the comparison ended. The entire camp was surrounded by rolls of barbed-wire fencing. At the corners of the camp compound and approximately every 100 yards between, there were posten boxes or towers with armed guards. There were 13 huts in the west compound, with a Luftwaffe Lager officer in charge.

Each barracks-like structure had 12 rooms, 26 feet by 15 feet and 10 feet high. The two windows opposite the door provided the only ventilation and natural light for this musty-smelling room. In time, we would not notice the stale air. Atky — Darrell Atkinson, Jim Taylor, and I joined the 12 in the room. In a way they were glad to see us, and they welcomed us because they knew we would share in the KP duties. On the other hand, this meant three more bodies in an already crowded room. Little did we know the Germans would add another five a few days later. The other members of the Cradle Crew, with whom I had flown in the Halifax bomber, were all sergeants. As noncommissioned officers they were billeted in the next hut, living under similar conditions.

Along one wall of the barracks there were six three-tiered bunks. The opposite side of the room had two double-tiered bunks, and the balance of the area on that side was our makeshift kitchen and stove. In front of the windows, where we ate all our meals, there were two picnic-style tables with benches. Counters with cabinets underneath divided the kitchen from the sleeping area. Food was stored in the cabinets. Buckets and cans were stored wherever it was convenient. The stove was used only for cooking, not heating. We were given small supplies of coal briquettes, which were never sufficient, and we invariably supplemented them with torn-up parcel boxes, making cooking a real chore. We did have knives, forks, and spoons. The knives had normal handles, but the blades had been partially broken to ensure that no one could injure or stab one of the guards.

Privacy was nonexistent. Throughout the compound there were numerous latrines that had 50 seats. The Germans emptied them weekly.

At night the entire camp was floodlighted, and the shutters were closed on the windows of each hut. At the 2100 hour curfew the only light, which was in the center of the room, was turned off. When the curfew siren sounded, the doors were closed. Anyone visiting in another hut spent the night where he was. Anyone attempting to venture out at night would be shot on sight. The huts were one to two feet off the ground, and the night guards roamed the camp with unfriendly German shepherd dogs. We found many evidences that the dogs had gone under our hut, and we felt sure they wore microphones around their necks to pick up any loose conversations that might be going on in the rooms after lights out. These elevated buildings made easier the Germans' search for tunnel construction. The elevation also made the buildings very cold in the winter, when the wind swept underneath.

Our slatted bunk beds had no mattresses or ticks, but they did have two blankets, which we could use in a variety of combinations: one over and one under, two under with none over, or two over with nothing on the slats. When we used this latter combination, by morning we felt that every slat had left an imprint on our backsides; usually it had. That April in Pomerania there were many cold nights, and with no heat in the room we did whatever we could to keep from freezing.

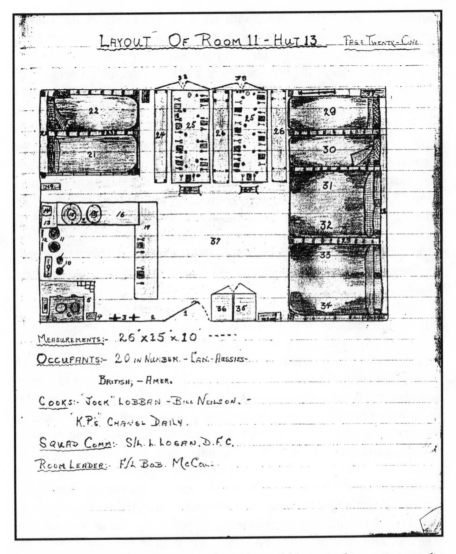

LAYOUT OF ROOM 11 - HUT 13   Page Twenty-One

MEASUREMENTS:- 26' x 15' x 10' ------
OCCUPANTS:- 20 IN NUMBER. - CAN.- AUSSIES-
          BRITISH; — AMER.
COOKS:- "JOCK" LOBBAN - BILL NEILSON. -
          K.P's. CHANGE DAILY.
SQUAD COMM:- S/L. L. LOGAN, D.F.C.
ROOM LEADER:- F/L. BOB. McCain.

At first it seemed strange to us that we would have to do our own cooking, but when we considered the facilities and the manpower the Germans would have needed to feed 9,000 prisoners, it made sense that we should do our own. Most of us were lucky if we knew how to make toast and boil water. Those who wanted to eat, quickly learned to cook.

The Germans awoke us early, at 0645 hours, for the first of two roll calls each day. The second was at 1630 hours. These were called Appells. Actually the Germans were tallying the number of prisoners in each hut.

"Key To Room Plan"

1.	Door To Room	19.	Red Cross Box For Personal Effects
2.	Wooden Pre-Fabricated Walls	20.	Personal Clothes Hanging On Wall
3.	Drying Towels Hanging On Walls	21.	Tom's Bed With Myself & Jock On Tiers Below
4.	Box For Empty Tins	22.	Rex's " " Jack & Bill " " e
5.	Concrete Floor For Stove	23.	Bunks 3 Tiers High – No Straw Or Mattresses
6.	Cooking Stove – Two Hot Plates – One Oven	24.	Wooden Bench At Side Of Table
7.	Chimney – Wall In Corner Is Brick	25.	Two Wooden Tables
8.	Coal Box – Large Red Cross Box	26.	Two Benches Made With Ramsey Stools
9.	Stick Box – " " " "	27.	Two Wooden Stools
10.	Two Tall Drinking-Water Cans	28.	Wooden Shelf For Personal Property
11.	Two Buckets	29.	Jeff's Bed With MacKay Below – Bottom Vacan
12.	Two Cake Tins Hanging On Wall	30.	Lee's " " Atky Below – " "
13.	Shelf For Tin Cups & Plates – R.C. Boxes	31.	Moon's " " Roger " " "
14.	Knife, Fork & Spoon Box – On Top Of Above	32.	Tiger's " " Bob " " "
15.	Two Aluminum Bowls	33.	MacDonald's " Jim " & Smith Below Him
16.	Wooden Counter	34.	Bob's " "Bill " "Spike " "
17.	Serving Table With Shelves For Food	35.	Cupboard For Firewood
18.	Oblong Tin Plate Made From Tin Cans German Aluminum Fork & Spoon	36.	" " Soap, Toilet Paper, Etc.
		37.	Floor – Dusty – Tongue & Groove Boarding
		38.	Windows

They lined us up in columns of five on the parade square because it was easier for them to count us that way. An earlier attempt to use a turnstile outside each hut turned out to be a disaster for the guards. The Kriegies went out the front door through the turnstile and returned through the back door. They would then repeat the process and make a second turn through the turnstile. We were to do what we were told but were not to go out of our way to be helpful. I do not know what count they produced, but they never repeated the process. I often wondered what would have happened if they had come up short on a roll call. Where would they have started to look? Would it have given the guards something to do?

After roll call we took our turns at cooking, but it was not long before we all agreed that Jock Lobban and Bill Neilson were the most proficient, and they seemed to like doing it. They did a great job with the few utensils they had to work with, the minimal fuel supply, and the limited food resources. They made some delicious, interesting creations such as prune pie. However, no one was overlooked for cleanup detail. We all had our turn at kitchen patrol. It is interesting how the body craves certain items when they are not found in the regular diet. I recall stealing and sucking on sugar cubes. Apparently there was not enough sugar in our diet, and the lone D-Bar did not make up for this deficiency. I cannot imagine considering sucking on a sugar cube today.

We wrote letters to our loved ones back home, but we wondered if they were ever received. None of mine reached my fiancee or my family. We did not expect to receive mail, having been there but a short time, but we looked forward to receiving our weekly Red Cross parcels. Most of them came from the United States, but we did receive one from Canada. The contents were basically the same. The Red Cross truck would arrive and under German guard supervision would unload just enough parcels for our compound. In some cases the parcels had been opened, but generally there was nothing missing. The guards must have been sorely tempted to steal some of the American cigarettes. Not being a smoker, I was always eager to trade off my cigarettes to a Kriegie who would trade almost any other item for some additional cigarettes.

I found out later that Colonel Zemke had negotiated a deal with the German Kommandant whereby a truck manned by Kriegies and two German guards with machine guns would drive to Lubeck to pick up the parcels shipped by the Swedish Red Cross. The parcels were then stored in the Flak School just outside our camp — under guard. There was always the danger they could be stolen by the local inhabitants. According to German regulations, these parcels could not be stored in the camp. One of our Kriegie officers kept the inventory, and though some of the parcels were taken, on the whole the pilferage was minimal. There was an indirect benefit for the Germans in the camp, because the more Red Cross parcels that were made available for the prisoners, the less food the Germans had to furnish from their own limited food supply. But there was a danger to the Kriegies driving the truck to Lubeck, because Allied fighter planes might strafe them, not realizing who they were. To my knowledge this never happened, but it was always a concern. I am still amazed that the guards did not pilfer our Red Cross parcels, because the contents were prized black market items. Possibly the camp kommandant was a disciplinarian who forbade theft by his soldiers.

I cannot recall the entire contents of the parcels, but the articles were all practical. Besides five packages of cigarettes in each, we had a large D-Bar of dark chocolate. This was the "pound sterling" of the camp — the medium of exchange. Prunes, sugar cubes, powdered milk, and coarse soap were mainstays. In one week we could never use the entire bar of soap. One prisoner traded for the excess soap and started up a laundry business, taking chits from the guys. I do not imagine that he was ever able to cash these in after he got home, but it kept him busy and passed the time.

The meals we had in the Dulag Luft were the same as those given to the German soldiers, not an exciting bill of fare. At Stalag Luft 1, the small amount of German food provided was prepared in a central kitchen by POW volunteers and distributed to the compounds once a day — potatoes, turnips, beets, and cabbage. Barley soup and black bread were always on the menu.

The black bread must have had sawdust for its main ingredient. The barley was like porridge or oatmeal. Each room had the responsibility of providing a large pan or bowl sufficient to hold the barley needs of the total number of men in the room. One of the Kriegies stood guard at the door of the hut, and when the German wagon came along with the barley supply, he would shout, "Bowls out for barley!"

Each room representative would make sure he got a sufficient amount for everyone in his room. The barley was somewhat flat tasting, but it did fill us up.

From time to time one of our fellow prisoners would come to our room and say that he had talked to a guard and if we were interested he could get us some onions or some other "goody" for supper. This, however, would cost each of us a package of cigarettes. American cigarettes were a premium item with the guards because the German cigarettes were in short supply and were very dry. To maintain the demand, when the POWs finished a cigarette, they were supposed to GI each butt — that is, tear the butt apart and sprinkle the tobacco on the ground. Sometimes, though, they would forget. It was amusing to watch a guard spot a butt on the ground, wander over to it, pretend to tie his shoelace or brush some dirt off the bottom of his trousers, and swiftly garner the butt. The Germans would collect these butts and roll their own cigarettes from them.

The senior Allied officers in the camp were not happy when we used our excess items from the parcels to bribe the guards for food. They preferred that these items be used to acquire other necessities, such as dry cell batteries for the secret radios.

Besides our weekly food parcels, the Red Cross was able to provide us with other necessities, such as books, blankets, and uniform clothing.

Other than the two roll calls daily there was nothing demanded of us by the Germans. We would go for walks around the compound and look through the barbed wire at the Luftwaffe Anti-Aircraft and Flak School, where German girls trained to be searchlight and radar operators and to do other tasks to relieve the military. When they marched they always sang. Watching and listening to these young girls was about the height of our entertainment.

From the International YMCA we received sports gear and hobby equipment. Without the YMCA and the Red Cross we would have gone mad. The Germans were smart enough to sense this. And they knew that if we were playing baseball or soccer, there was little likelihood we could plan an escape.

We were all competitive enough to enjoy a baseball game pitting one hut against another. When we were not playing we were cheering. Among the Americans we had a cross section of life from the U.S., and throughout the camp we had some pretty good ballplayers, professional musicians, and other talented people. I recall one afternoon baseball game between an American team and a British team. The game was suddenly halted when the British players demanded tea be served, right on the playing field. The American team protested. The umpire pondered the problem for a moment and then announced: "According to British rules tea is served. According to American rules no tea is served. My hands are tied. Still, it's a helluva idea, so let's all stop for tea."

We had to entertain ourselves to pass the time, and physical exercise helped us sleep easier and longer. (We often took a siesta in the afternoon.) On wet days, which were few, gin rummy and bridge games flourished. This recreation took place inside the barbed-wire entanglements. The camp was protected with the posten boxes —the towers on stilts — every so many feet, between which were heavy rolls of barbed wire. They were manned by guards with machine guns. About 15 or 20 feet inside the barbed wire was a warning wire. Anyone who attempted to go between the warning wire and the barbed wire would be shot without question. In fact, it was not a good idea to touch the warning wire. There might be a trigger-happy guard in the tower. Occasionally during a baseball or soccer game the ball would end up inside the restricted area. We were never allowed to retrieve it; we had to wait for one of the roaming guards to come along and recover it before the game could continue. I played in many of these games, and we learned to handle the interruptions.

After six years of war the German military was probably hurting for qualified, physically fit personnel for front-line duty, resulting in the older, less able soldiers being used for assignments such as prison guard. Their primary function was to make sure we did not escape. We called all the guards "Goons." For the most part, though, they left us to ourselves. Generally, the German military was respectful of the Allied military. Because we had been interrogated earlier, no attempts were made to question us further while we were in the camp.

"George," the camp guard we had met on arrival at Stalag Luft 1, was the stereotypical German guard, fitting nicely into this laissez faire category. He stood about five feet, ten inches, with his swarthy features somewhat hidden by the jaunty German hat and formfitting greatcoat. He did what he had to do and did not make many waves. He was highly visible as a roaming guard in our compound, and we learned he was familiar with Saskatchewan, a midwestern Canadian province, because he had been a Canadian wheat farmer. At the "request" of the Führer he had returned to Germany to help liberate his homeland. If he had refused, his parents, still living in Germany, would have been interned.

Chapter 4

Tarmac and Training Start-Up

*I*N EARLY FEBRUARY 1943, the Initial Training School
apparently was not ready to accept us at this particular
time, so off we went for Tarmac duty at the Bombing and
Gunnery School at Mountain View, Ontario. Tarmac duty
covered anything from being temporarily assigned to the military police, to sitting out in a Nissen hut just off the bombing
range and plotting the practice smoke bombs as they were
dropped on the target area by the bombing and gunnery aircrew
training personnel. There was still plenty of snow on the ground
at the Mountain View facility on Lake Ontario, and at this time

of year blizzards often blew in off the lake. All these assignments became boring, and the snow and cold made some of them extremely unpleasant.

Two of my buddies, Bob Brown and "Uncle" Mac Ault, were assigned to military police duties on the midnight to 8:00 a.m. shift. "Uncle" Mac had a noticeable stutter, which became accentuated when he was nervous or excited. One particular night the wind was blowing and there was a blinding snowstorm. Mac and Bob each had to check some of the hangars. It seems Mac went onto the roof of one, and, unknown to him, Bob climbed up from the other side. In the blinding snow, Mac did not recognize Bob; at a distance he could only see someone moving on the roof of the hangar. He drew his revolver and said, "SSSSSTTTTOPPP! Sttttep ffforwwward thththree pppaces and iddddentifffy yyyourself!" Bob realized it was Mac, but the stuttering caused him to laugh so hard Mac damn near shot him before he could respond.

Mac slept in the bunk above me, and when he came off duty in the morning, he was a sight to behold. His mustache was completely iced up and he was nearly frozen. This was degrading to Mac, who was usually so dapper. He firmly believed he was a charmer with the ladies, and he kept his mustache trimmed to perfection. When we were at the Wet P course in Montreal, we hung the "Uncle" moniker on him because he was an uncle to all the ladies at the Lady Davis' House. If there was any consolation in Tarmac duty, it was that everyone who would eventually be in aircrew would experience a stint at one of these training schools doing the "Joe jobs."

At last came the posting to the Initial Training School in mid-March. At this point we all felt that we were finally getting down to serious business. Although there were Initial Training Schools in the East to which we could have been sent, we were moved from Mountain View, Ontario, by train to Saskatoon, Saskatchewan, reaching the heart of the prairies in three nights and two days.

I was not familiar with the other branches of the military, but it appeared that the RCAF moved the Eastern trainees to the West, and the Western trainees to the East. This was an excellent opportunity for the Easterners to learn more about the West and vice versa. More importantly, it became the starting ground for many romances which later bloomed into marriages, mostly after the war. I was no exception. In Saskatoon I met Sarah Wiebe, one of nine daughters in the Wiebe household, which also had three sons. Twelve children in one family overwhelmed me at first, but

I got used to it. They were all very close. I met Sarah through her sister Margo, and when I did, that was the end of my playing the field.

At this point in our training we were promoted to Leading Aircraftsmen, and as aircrew trainees we wore a white wedge in our caps. It appeared reasonably certain we would wind up in aircrew, either as pilots or navigators. Washouts in this course usually ended up in ground crew.

Our billeting for this Initial Training Course was in the Saskatoon Normal School. However, our classes were held daily in the Saskatoon Technical School, some distance from the Normal School. Every morning the RCAF marching band would muster outside the Normal School and parade us across town to the Technical School. At noon they marched us back again and repeated the performance again in the afternoon. Without them it would have been a boring exercise, but with them we found it somewhat enjoyable. The drummers were permitted to use some imagination in creating rhythms not normally used for marching purposes.

The Royal Canadian Air Force curriculum for aircrew officially started at the Initial Training School, where we were exposed to a series of studies leading up to a battery of tests to determine where our particular talents might best be utilized. The instructors believed I had pilot potential and in mid-June sent me to Virden, a small station in southern Manitoba. Virden was a flat prairie town where the wind always blew, and the hot summer days caused the deHavilland D.H. 82 Tiger Moth, our first training aircraft, to make many of the aircrew trainees airsick on more than one occasion.

At this Elementary Flying Training School (EFTS) we were divided into two classes. Those who flew in the morning had ground school in the afternoon. The morning ground school group flew in the early evening. The extreme turbulence from noon to three o'clock was too much for even the instructors, so we had siesta time during those hours. On alternate days, the classes were reversed.

During the entire training program in Canada and overseas I was involved in three crashes. Like a cat, perhaps, I used three of my nine lives. The first crash occurred at Virden on July 7, 1943. After some 6 hours and 20 minutes of dual instruction on the Tiger Moth biplane, my instructor,

Art McKenna climbing aboard a Tiger Moth.

Flight Sergeant McDonald, believed that I was ready to fly solo. Although I had been having some difficulty with my takeoffs, my landings were satisfactory, so McDonald thought I could give it a "go."

"Mac" McDonald was a big guy. Hell, he was fat — and when he flew with me he sat in the front seat of the Tiger Moth.

My solo takeoff went well and I was elated. I sang to myself as I made the circuit and started my approach. Everything was going too well, however. Without Mac up front, this small aircraft responded too quickly when I gently pulled back on the stick; before I knew it I had stalled and spun in from about 50 feet. The two wings took the brunt of the crash. I was unhurt, but mad at myself for not having made an allowance for the drastic change in weight. Mac came running out. When he saw that I was okay, he said, "You owe me a Coke for that one."

We made another dual circuit the following morning. Afterwards, I went solo without further mishap.

The flying assignments were all numbered. Once we had soloed, when we entered the flight room we would check to see our practice lesson for that day. The one that frightened us most was number 10: solo spins. Those who drew number 10 for the first time invariably asked, "What if the aircraft doesn't come out of the spin?"

The instructor always replied: "Let go of the stick and it will come out by itself" — not a particularly comforting thought when one is spinning 3,000 feet above the ground! Frightening as it was, I managed the first attempt all right, and after a while I sort of enjoyed practicing spins.

One particularly windy day, Bill Randall, one of the older members of our class, had taken off in an extremely strong head wind, and he was having trouble landing. The Tiger Moth had a very low airspeed to begin with, and as Bill made his approach to the grass airfield into the strong head wind, the aircraft appeared to be hanging in space, almost like a dragonfly. Bill bounced a couple times, panicked, opened the throttle, and climbed to about 1,000 feet. He did this a second and a third time, and the same thing happened. Many of the guys on the ground started making bets he was going to jump. One of my buddies suggested that on his next approach we should try to jump onto the wings, because the aircraft's ground speed would be very slow on his approach. I went along with him. When Bill approached, he had to wonder what the hell those two clowns on the ground were up to. Wasn't he having enough trouble just trying to land this damn thing without having to dodge guys on the ground? My buddy was the first to jump onto the wing, and as he did, Bill hit the rudder and effectively took the Tiger Moth out of the wind but flipped my classmate about 15 feet through the air. He was unhurt, and Bill was happy to be down. Bill finally asked to be washed out and placed in another part of aircrew.

Teaching had to be a boring assignment for the instructors at EFTS. The Tiger Moth was an obsolete biplane with little airspeed. It had a relic of a communication system between the two cockpits: a tube with a funnel at each end between the student and the instructor. It is easy to imagine the instructor taking "40 winks" as he sat alone in the front cockpit, with no air conditioning, and with the convection currents causing the little aircraft to bounce around on hot June and July days in Manitoba. On several occasions Mac gave me instructions to perform an exercise, and after I had been doing it for an unreasonable length of time I noticed his head slumped forward in the front cockpit. I would call through the tube in a loud voice and awaken him. His head would jerk, and he would call out for me to do some other exercise. He never commented on the dozing.

On July 21 I took my 20-hour check with Pilot Officer Currie, a miserable, crabby instructor who made me quite nervous during the testing procedure. Suddenly he closed the throttle from his forward position and asked me: "What field did you pick for a forced landing?"

I had not picked out any field, but I was not about to tell him that, so I quickly pointed to one off my starboard wing. There was a little more to it than just picking out a field. In such a small aircraft, determining the wind direction was important because the approach to the field had to be upwind. There was no windsock for a guide, so the pilot had to make use of whatever was available. Often the smoke from a farmhouse would help. Another clue was that cattle in a field invariably face into the wind. (Even today when I see cattle in a field I smile when I see them all facing the same direction.)

Unfortunately, in my rattled condition my forced landing procedure was anything but perfect. Frankly, it stank. Currie had me so nervous I forgot what little I knew about forced landing. The procedure did not call for us to actually land in the field, but to fly with a dead stick until we were within 50 feet of the ground, when we opened the throttle; with the power back on, we climbed to 2,000 feet for our return to base.

Currie let me know in no uncertain terms what a lousy demonstration I had made. I felt sure this was the end of my pilot career. Fortunately, my instructor was not overly fond of Mr. Currie either, and he paid no attention to the report, except to give me some additional dual training on forced landings.

Four days later, on a beautiful, quiet evening, Flying Officer Pollock asked if I would like to go along with him. We did some spins, and he complimented my performance. Then he asked if I had done any loops or rolls. Since I had not, he suggested I tighten my flying harness; then he showed me how it was done. I tried a few and did reasonably well. Then we went down on the deck and proceeded to curdle the milk out of a herd of cows. I was having a great time when we climbed to 3,000 feet again, and he asked me to try a forced landing. This time I gave one of my better performances. We tried it several times, with the same result. After more low-level flying we headed back to the station.

I found out later this was my repeat 20-hour check. This time my marks were above standard. When it came time for my 60-hour check, I was a little more prepared, and Pilot Officer Wickware gave me high marks.

We were fortunate that during our stint at Virden there were no serious accidents, but quite a number of the students in our class did "wash out." I recall one such incident in particular. After every practice session, Jake

Finestein, a short, stocky student, would take off his flying helmet and comment, "Was I terrific today! I couldn't do anything wrong!"

I was never quite sure whether he was overly excited with his flying or was nervous and made such a remark to hide it. He said this so many times that we began to believe him. On this particular day, however, he took off with his instructor for a checkout. On his return he was downcast. I asked him what had happened. He replied, "When we taxied out I felt the instructor would give me control for the takeoff. He didn't. We started to climb to several thousand feet and I expected at any moment he would say, 'You've got control.' He didn't. We started some exercises, and I felt sure this was it and I would hear, 'You've got control.' I didn't. We headed back to the station. Surely now he would say, 'You've got control.' No way. We started in for the landing, and about 100 feet from the ground he said, 'You've got control.'

"I was so mad by this time I said, 'Stuff it, you've still got control.' And now I'm washed out."

After eight weeks our class was apparently ready for Service Flying Training School (SFTS). Approximately half of us would advance to training on twin-engine Cessna Cranes at Saskatoon; the balance would move on to a single-engine school at another location to receive their wings on Harvard Trainers. It would take another five months of training before graduation, when I would receive my wings.

The class was excited on September 27, when we returned to Saskatoon, the same city where we had taken our Initial Training. Whereas Virden was a small town, Saskatoon was one of the larger cities in the province of Saskatchewan. I was doubly excited, because this would allow me to continue romancing Sarah Wiebe.

At the time it seemed like a big step from the single-engine Tiger Moth to the twin-engine Cessna Crane. The Cessna was a dual-controlled aircraft, so the instructor sat alongside the student instead of up front as in the Tiger Moth. It had a longer range, and our cross-country exercises required more navigational skill than we had needed on the smaller Tiger Moth. For the instructors it had to be a bore teaching class after class of trainees. My instructor, Flying Officer Hobson, like Flight Sergeant

The Cessna Crane.

The Crane in echelon port formation.

Mac McDonald, would often catch 40 winks while I was busy watching my instruments. I could never really tell if he was asleep or not, for his arms always hung at his sides. The gas cocks were under his seat, and on one cross-country he quietly turned off one of the cocks. Before I knew it the starboard engine began to sputter. Not knowing what he had done, I thought we had run out of petrol. I was able to stabilize the aircraft on the one engine, but not before he had climbed all over me for not being alert to the fact that I had not noticed the fuel gauge was reading "EMPTY." At the time I was not impressed, but it was a valuable lesson; and in the future I took more care with all the gauges in the aircraft.

My student partner at EFTS was Art McKenna from Montreal, Quebec. We became fast friends. We both soloed about the same time, nine hours and five minutes. The Tiger Moth had a fixed undercarriage; in other words, it did not retract on takeoff. It also had a turn and bank indicator.

The Cessna was a twin-engine aircraft with a retractable undercarriage. On the panel it had an artificial horizon, a miniature aircraft appearing on a single line. In this manner you could determine if you were in a dive, in a climb, or if one of your wings was not level. Simple as it may sound, it took some time before we had mastered it.

At #4 SFTS we had our first official experience in formation flying. Only three aircraft were involved, and we took turns being the leader and moving from one wing position to another. This was known as echelon port or echelon starboard formations.

In our earlier training on the Tiger Moth we had learned spins, rolls, and loops. When we started into one of these procedures, we dived the aircraft until we reached 115 miles per hour. Then we pulled back on the stick and performed one of the three exercises. There was no way we were going to deliberately loop or roll the Cessna. In my opinion, it was a fragile aircraft, and I was dubious we could ever recover from a spin. I certainly hoped I would never have to try.

December 10, 1943, in Saskatoon on a bitter-cold winter's day, I received my wings on the Cessna Crane at #4 SFTS. It was not uncommon for the temperature to be 30 below; in fact, the year before it had dropped to 56 below for a day or two. We avoided going outside, where it hurt to breathe.

The graduation ceremony was impressive for three reasons. First, we received our wings. Second, the Canadian Pacific Railway, my employer before joining the RCAF, gave my mother a pass to come by train from

Ottawa for the graduation. Though she was not happy about my being in the service, I am sure she was proud to see her oldest son graduate. Last but not least, our entire class was made pilot officers. In our excitement we rushed out and bought our officer uniforms, then walked around downtown Saskatoon looking for some NCOs and acknowledging their salutes. I was "flying" particularly high that evening because Sarah and I became engaged.

After graduation our entire class went on leave, allowing all of us to get home for Christmas. When leave was completed our class was posted to a godforsaken location at Maitland, Nova Scotia, a military facility on the East Coast, on the Bay of Fundy. Apparently someone at RCAF headquarters had decided that all aircrew were in poor physical condition and needed some commando-like training.

We were placed in the hands of the Army for conditioning. Part of our training included gunnery practice; for want of a better target they had us shoot at the large chunks of ice floating in the Bay of Fundy.

The barracks at the facility were not the best, and the roads at the camp were unpaved. The notorious Maritime red clay was a disaster to march in — and virtually impossible to get out of our clothes. At one time the military had planned to make this facility an airport, but because of the horrendous weather (principally fog) the plan was discarded. The Army — both enlisted men and officers — reveled in running the pants off the Air Force personnel. Whenever one of us tried to dog it, the whole group would be taken on a hike with full packs on our backs.

We were delighted in early 1944 when this stint finally was over and we were en route to Halifax, Nova Scotia, for deployment overseas. Coincidentally, the boat we sailed on, the *Louis Pasteur*, left on March 31, 1944, exactly one year to the day before I was shot down over Germany. No big deal, just a coincidence.

We did not travel in a convoy on the Atlantic, because the *Louis Pasteur* was considered fast enough to go it alone. En route the captain called for some gunnery practice, so a target was dropped off on a raft behind our vessel. The crew commenced shooting at it, and we could see the shells ricocheting off the water. No one hit the target. Let me say no one came *close* to hitting the target, which did not leave us with a warm feeling that we were in safe hands en route to England.

If there was one time when I was happy I was an officer, it had to be on the trip overseas. The enlisted men aboard slept in hammocks in the hold of the ship, and their food rations left a lot to be desired. Frankly, their quarters looked comparable to slave ship quarters. On several occasions I saw the NCOs at mealtime. They had what I can best describe as a giant sardine can for a dinner plate, and whatever they were fed was eaten off that plate — not very appetizing, to say the least.

The officers shared cabins. They were fed in the dining rooms. Many of them got seasick on the voyage, so it was not unusual to eat alone at the table. When we did, we managed to secret out the meals of those on the sick list and give them to our buddies below.

We landed at Liverpool and went by train to Bournemouth, a beautiful city on the south coast of England. We were billeted in the many hotels in this internationally known resort city. We were shocked to see how these hotels had been allowed to deteriorate. Servicemen who had stayed there had completely destroyed what had once been the pride of southern England. And though it cost a great deal to restore these buildings after the war, it was eventually done. Bournemouth was a holding point for aircrew until it was decided where they were needed.

One of the major disappointments for me during 1943 was my assignment, May 16, to an Advanced Flying Unit at Church Lawford in Warwickshire, England, where we would be trained to become flying instructors. If the RCAF had planned to make me a flying instructor, I could have remained in Canada, where I had become engaged just prior to the overseas posting. Unfortunately, I had no say in the matter.

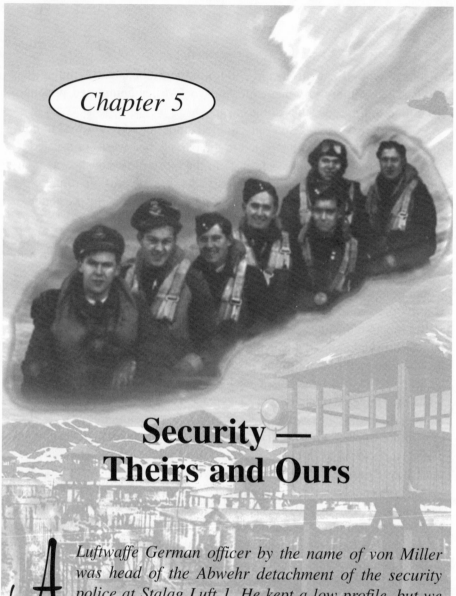

Chapter 5

Security — Theirs and Ours

A Luftwaffe German officer by the name of von Miller was head of the Abwehr detachment of the security police at Stalag Luft 1. He kept a low profile, but we knew these officers were never far away.

High water during the winter months had made tunneling at the camp very dangerous and virtually impossible in the spring of 1945. Unknown to us at the time, the Germans had seismographic equipment that would fix on underground noises. Von Miller would let some of the tunnels be built almost to completion, then pounce on them. It would frustrate and dishearten the prisoners, who, if caught, would end up in the Stubenarrest building (the "cooler") in solitary confinement. And von Miller committed prisoners from time to time for other crimes also.

No Red Cross parcels and only limited smoking were allowed in confinement. I wonder what happened to the parcels that were confiscated.

One of the assignments each of us in the hut took seriously was manning the front and back doors of our barracks. We took turns sitting on the stoop reading a book, and when a roaming guard came along we shouted, "On guard!"

Most of the time nothing of concern to our captors was going on inside the hut, but to protect ourselves we always announced the guard's arrival. Sometimes the lookout would become so engrossed in his book that he would not see the guard approaching. Often the guard would shout, "On guard!" then laugh. He thought it was funny.

But the assignment was very important because one of the Kriegies had built a receiving radio, which could pick up the BBC news broadcasts. He had taken a great risk in bribing several of the German guards for the parts he needed. The Germans must have had some idea what he was up to, and while they enjoyed the items the Kriegie had used to bribe them, there was no guarantee that they would not inform their superiors about what they thought he was doing. He built this radio in such a manner that, when completed, it looked like a commonplace object in the room. The Germans must have been able to determine in which hut the radio was located, because the hut experienced unexpected searches at all hours of the day and night. These investigations had to be unnerving, not only to the Kriegie who had built the radio, but to all the members of the room where it was located. To their credit, however, it was never found.

Each day this Kriegie would pick up the BBC news broadcasts at 1300 hours and 2100 hours and transcribe them completely. He called this paper the *Red Star*. Then he or one of his buddies would go inconspicuously from hut to hut, where the men would all gather in one room to hear the latest news. This was a terrific morale booster. Although the Germans gave us some information on the state of the war, we knew theirs was far from accurate. They had a large map in one of the open buildings, and on it was drawn where they believed (or where they wanted us to believe) the front lines were located. From time to time this was modified. But according to our BBC news broadcasts they were only fooling themselves.

We had learned that around D-Day, June 6, 1944, one of the newer

prisoners at the camp advised that the Voice of America programs contained encoded messages for the POWs. We also had been led to believe
that these messages, after being decoded, had some meaning for Group
Captain Cecil Weir. The Kriegies who had been in the camp the longest
believed that Weir had intentionally bailed out over enemy territory and
had allowed himself to be captured to ensure that Canadian and British
personnel did not make any unnecessary or poorly planned escape
attempts. Shortly after our arrival, in March 1945, the group captain had
told us that any attempt to escape would be foolhardy since the end of the
war was not far off.

We soon discovered that the best way to make the time pass quickly was
to become involved in something – besides playing baseball or soccer, we
could play cards, read, or reach into our imaginations and be creative. One
way to spend the day was to invent something that made our life easier in
the camp.

During one of our nightly strolls for exercise, Jim Taylor and I came
upon a Kriegie sitting on a stool, pedaling a contraption he had made out
of Klim cans. (The Klim cans, a part of every Red Cross parcel, contained
powdered milk. They were similar in shape and size to a one-pound coffee can.) Using the Klim can, a foot pedal he had made, and some string,
he had built a blower for heating a large can of water. With his invention
and two coal briquettes he could boil the can of water in half the time it
took on the stove, using only a fraction of the fuel — and he could read a
book at the same time!

Another diversion was to be part of a talent show. There were several
talent shows while I was in the camp; I recall one in particular. The International YMCA had supplied us with some musical instruments, and some
of the prisoners had been members of big-name dance bands. Some had
the ability to write original musical scores and arrangements. The orches-
tra they formed was no Benny Goodman or Artie Shaw, but considering
what they had to work with, the music they created was every bit as good.
Some of the men were fine vocalists, and with a few would-be comedians,
we had a show. I remember a few of the lines, all original material from
camp experiences:

Let me tell you about the Memel — He eats Spam.
Do you know what Spam is?
It's the Society For the Preservation and Annihilation of the Memel.

Not funny? To us it was hilarious. We had Spam as our main meat dish. At this same show, one Kriegie played a beautiful solo on a violin he had made from pieces of wood he had glued together, sanded, and finished with varnish he had secured from a bribed guard. The Red Cross had found him a bow.

And amidst all this, the roaming guards, if they understood English, usually watched to make sure we were not up to something.

Another Kriegie showed his creativity by designing a pair of wings with a parachute, with "P.O.W." inscribed in the center. (To be more accurate, it was scratched on.) He made a sand mold, then melted the metallic prune box lining, and *voilà*, he had an item he could trade or sell to other Kriegies. I still have the one I bought from him for a D-Bar.

During one of these talent shows I first heard a song that my mother and sister had written to me about while I was still on the squadron. They knew I loved popular music, since I had led a dance band before joining the service. It was ironic that I heard "Don't Fence Me In" for the first time when I was *fenced in*!

When we heard air raid sirens, we were confined to our barracks. We could hear Uncle Joe's guns in the southwest. Uncle Joe, of course, was Joseph Stalin, dictator of the USSR. From the *Red Star* information off the BBC news, we were aware that the Allied lines were somewhat dormant. They were not moving forward as quickly as we had hoped. It was the end of April 1945, and the Allies were some 60 miles west of our camp. On the other hand, the BBC news indicated that the Russians were moving forward, and we were anticipating that our release would come from them before our own troops could reach us. Our concern was that the Russians would not know where the camp was located and would start shelling our area. The information we had was that the front-line troops of the Russians were Cossacks, a rough and tough group, who would shoot first and then investigate. They were known to have their women fighting alongside them. Their military believed this was sound planning; they claimed to have a very low VD rate. Later we saw proof that the women were with the men — when they entered the camp.

During April 1945, the air-raid warnings had become more frequent. It was not always possible to hear the siren, and in several instances Kriegies were fired upon en route to the latrine or returning to their own huts. Apparently they had not heard the warning.

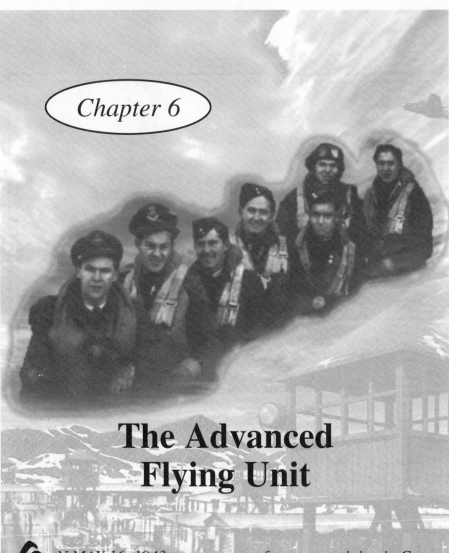

Chapter 6

The Advanced
Flying Unit

O N MAY 16, 1943, we were sent from our training in Canada to #18 Advanced Flying Unit at Church Lawford in
Warwickshire. This was a typical Royal Air Force station
located near Rugby, with its famous English school.
There were Canadian-run squadrons in Yorkshire, but all the
training stations in England were run totally by English Royal
Air Force personnel. Their discipline was somewhat more rigid,
but it gave us little concern. More importantly, we were once
again excited about actually sitting at the controls of an aircraft.
In appearance, the twin-engine Airspeed Oxford was similar to

An early model B-24 Liberator of the RAF. The Canadians later flew the more sophisticated Liberator IV on maritime patrols.

the twin-engine Cessna Crane we had graduated on at Saskatoon, but it seemed sturdier and safer.

At all these RAF stations our diet consisted mostly of mutton and Brussels sprouts. The Brussels sprouts were dispensed from a large container on the steam table, and what we did not eat one day would be served to us again the next. I did not eat Brussels sprouts again for 25 years. I had often told my buddies that if I ever had the chance I was going to land at an American operational station and get a decent meal. It was just a casual remark; I never believed it could come true. But it did.

One day I was doing a training exercise that required me to fly solo cross-country. My map was on a flimsy — a flat board with the map glued to it — and attached by a strap to my leg for easy access. The flight plan called for me to fly a rectangular pattern to destinations located at the very edge of the map. En route I was to practice single-engine procedure, switching off one engine yet maintaining straight and level flight, then reversing the procedure and doing the same with the other engine. The exercise also specified that I practice steep turns.

The first leg of the trip took me to Nottingham. Now everybody knows that Nottingham is the home of Robin Hood, Sherwood Forest, and Maid Marian. I decided to do my steep turn exercises over Sherwood Forest and keep an eye out for Maid Marian. The turns must have been steeper than I thought, because they resulted in toppling my gyro compass. The aircraft carried two compasses: a liquid one, which was 100 percent accurate but was not practical to change course on because it floated in a liquid and took some time to settle down, and a gyrocompass that responded immediately and was used to set course. The problem with the gyro was that it toppled or spun on extreme banking maneuvers and had to be reset against the liquid compass.

My search for Maid Marian had kept me so occupied that when I set course for my next destination I had not noticed the gyro topple, and had set course for the second leg of my exercise assuming the gyro compass to be accurate. Before I knew it I could see the North Sea in front of me, and I realized something was amiss. I checked the gyro against the liquid compass and saw my error. Without thinking, I reset the gyro with the liquid compass, then realized this was a mistake. If I had been alert, I would have turned 180 degrees on the gyro, which would have taken me back to Nottingham. Now I did not know where the hell I was! I was beyond the limits of my map. Trying to find a landmark that would get me back on my map was not in the cards. Aircraft flying at unreasonably low levels over some of these British facilities could provide an interesting target for some of the ground forces with itchy trigger fingers. In addition to this, I was running low on petrol.

Back in Western Canada if I became lost, it was a simple matter to follow a railroad track until I came to a grain elevator, and could fly low enough to read the name of the town written in large letters on its side. In England, however, the countryside was densely populated, with railroad tracks running in every direction, and there were no grain elevators to help me out. I decided to forget it and look for the American station.

Almost at that moment, I spotted a black B-24 Liberator off my starboard side. The black Liberators were usually on coastal command. If I could find where it came from, I would then have the American station where I might get that great meal. Sure enough, off to my right I could see an entire squadron of Liberators. I headed right for it. After requesting and receiving permission to land, I taxied up to the tower and reported in to the air control officers. I told them I was lost, and they notified my station — which, by the way, was not too far away. The tower officer offered to get me a sandwich from their mess, which was disappointing, to say the least. At that moment, a young Chinese sergeant jumped up and said, "Sir, the mess hall is open, and we could run you over to it if you wish."

This kid was definitely going places! I gratefully accepted, and a jeep picked me up and took me to the mess hall. Dinner had not yet started, but right in front of me there was a large container full of pork chops. I took only three; I did not want to hurt their feelings. Applesauce and apple pie finished the meal. With a full stomach and a tank full of American petrol, I headed for my base, where I was given hell for having taken so long to return the aircraft. But I wasn't bothered by the criticism, though my buddies accused me of making up the story.

On another occasion, while still at Church Lawford, I was flying alone, practicing forced landings. The procedure called for the pilot to shut off the engine at 3,000 feet, select a suitable field in which to land, and attempt to make a landing without the use of power. This required "S"-like maneuvers until I was about 50 feet from the ground, when I would put the power back on, climb again to 3,000 feet, and repeat the exercise. It was a beautiful sunny day, and I practiced this particular exercise several times before returning to the station.

Especially proud of my forced-landing skills, I was surprised to be called before the chief flying instructor as soon as I had landed. He immediately started to ask me about where I had been and what I had been doing. I was given no explanation for the inquiries. When the discussion was over I was informed that I was grounded until further notice and that I had to appear before the wing commander. The following day I met with Wing Commander Sloan, who advised me that the commanding officer of our station had appointed him to hold a hearing on me. Apparently a complaint had been received from another station that two Oxfords had flown low over their station and had almost collided with a Wellington, which was about to land. The flying control officer assumed that the pilot of the other aircraft and I were doing a low-level exercise, and he requested that future aircraft be routed away from their station. The WingCo took down the particulars on what exercises I had been doing the day before and stated that an officer from the station in question would be over the next day to give us his report of the situation. I asked whether I would be allowed to question him and was given permission to do so.

When the officer arrived, he stated that an Oxford had flown within 50 feet of the tower. According to him, the Oxford had the same number on its side as the one I had been flying.

I asked him, "Did this aircraft have any distinguishing markings, other than it was painted yellow?"

"Absolutely not," He replied.

When he left I told the WingCo that I had been flying a "day-night" kite (aircraft) with red engine nacelles (the housing of the engine), and that the pilot he saw was someone else. Normally this aircraft would be reserved for students working with their instructors and practicing instrument training while "under the hood" (a covering placed over the windshield in front of the pilot). On that particular day, the plane was not needed for that type of assignment, so it was signed out for me to use, like all other training aircraft. All aircraft we flew up through the Advanced Training Unit were painted yellow, and because they claimed I had the only Oxford in all of England with that number, flying alone, I would have had a difficult time defending myself. The fact that I was flying a day-night aircraft was a godsend. The WingCo was pleased, because he believed this would definitely absolve me from any wrongdoing.

The commanding officer held the report for several days longer than necessary, which permitted all my buddies to go on leave while I had to await his decision. I was finally called before him and found him to be in a combative mood. He held up a book and asked me if I knew what it was. I replied, "Yes Sir. It is *K R Air*, the rules of flying."

He put the book down and lit into me about the incident. Not only would he not admit he was wrong in accusing me, but he also felt that the fact that I was flying a day-night aircraft was insignificant. Since my innocence could only be supported by this fact, I was upset. I reminded him that if I had flown over the station in question at 10,000 feet, the flying control officer would have been able to see the red engine nacelles. After much huffing and puffing, he finally conceded that I had been unjustly accused. I believe that if he had had his way, I would have been court-martialed.

There was one other noteworthy incident while I was at Church Lawford. Our flight training was almost completed, and it was time for my instrument check, which was done by the Chief Flying Instructor, Flight Lieutenant Cow, a typical, straight-laced British officer, who made one uncomfortable. We called him "Holy."

"Holy" was quite a taskmaster. For the instrument test it was imperative we use a "day-night" kite with dual-control, so that the pilot's vision could be blocked to simulate night flying. After we had climbed to the desired altitude I took over control "under the hood." I could not see outside, and my eyes were fastened on the instrument panel. "Holy" directed me to do certain exercises relying totally on the instruments. Of course, he had complete visibility. The red engine nacelles on these aircraft provided a warning to other pilots that this pilot was "under the hood" and they must keep clear. Apparently I performed quite well, and "Holy" said he would like to try something with me that he had have never attempted before, adding, "If you don't wish to do it I'll understand."

"What have you got in mind?"

He wanted to "talk me down," while still under the hood, to a landing on the grassy field at our station. Oxfords do not make landings like the aircraft of today, which make wheel or tripod landings. The Oxford makes a three-pointer, or stalled landing. I thought this could be very interesting. I was too young to recognize the danger, even with an experienced pilot telling me what moves to make.

Throughout the exercise I was unaware of where I was, but I accepted the challenge. "Holy" would give me instructions to turn onto a particular heading and descend at a given number of feet per minute. When the altimeter got below 1,000 feet, it was evident to me we were making our approach to the field. Surprisingly, I had no real fear with the exercise and made one of my better landings under his experienced eye. At no point did he attempt to touch the stick or interfere with my flying.

He was elated. I think he thought that he should get some kind of medal for his accomplishment. My participation in this experience was apparently inconsequential to him.

Church Lawford did not have Standard Beam Approach capabilities, so we were transferred temporarily to a Polish operational squadron in Faldingsworth, Lincolnshire, which did. We had to dovetail our training with their operating schedule.

The Standard Beam Approach was a combination of instrument flying and a radio beam, which produced a steady hum in the pilot's headset if the pilot was exactly on course on a specified frequency. The steady hum was known as the cone of silence. If the aircraft drifted to one side, the pilot heard a "dah dit" repeated. If the plane drifted to the other side he heard "dit dah" repeated. During the descent, if the pilot drifted off course he made the necessary corrections to bring the plane back until it picked up the steady hum. This was not as simple as it may appear. When the pilot made a correction, the "dit dah" sound would melt into the hum, at which time he would make a minor correction to keep on course. If overdone, the aircraft would soon be back into the "dit dah" area, or would pass through the hum and onto the other side. This corrective action took place quickly while the aircraft descended through clouds. In dense clouds, it was possible this procedure would have to be followed until the aircraft was 100 feet, from the ground. At 100 feet the pilot *hoped* he would be able to see the landing strip. This instrument approach training was similar to the day-night training taken at Church Lawford.

Because the British Isles is not a large land mass, it was conceivable that extreme weather conditions could fog in all stations at the same time. While this was unlikely, we prepared for the possibility. One might ask, however, and reasonably so, what *would* happen if all of England *was* blanketed by fog.

At a point called Downham Market, south of the Wash and due west of Norwich, was a station with "FIDO": Fog Investigation and Dispersal Operation. Simply stated, a series of pipes ran alongside the major runway with jet outlets, which could be fired up should it be necessary to use this facility in a dire emergency. The flames that would be emitted would set up an intense heat, which would lift the fog hopefully some 100 feet from the ground.

When crews were directed to land there, they would make their approach on the SBA (Standard Beam Approach). If it was carried out effectively, when they broke cloud they would be staring at the flames from pipes paralleling either side of the runway and be able to make their landing. There were several of these facilities, but they never received widespread use because of the extreme expense of the operation. Fortunately, the Cradle Crew never had to take advantage of them.

One of my buddies at Advanced Flying Unit was Howard "Rip" Riopelle. Rip was from my hometown of Ottawa. After the war he became a professional hockey player, playing forward on the Montreal Royals the year they won the Allen Cup, one step removed from the Stanley Cup, the most prized award in hockey. The following year he joined the Montreal

Canadiens and played with them for quite a few years. Rip was a room-mate in the same Nissen hut, and we became very good friends. On one occasion we were doing night navigational exercises. When Rip saw that his assignment for this particular night was a solo cross country, he went up to his instructor and said, "Say, so far I haven't done a dual night cross country, and you have me lined up to do a solo exercise. What do you want me to do? Go up and grope around?" He followed the remark with his highly contagious laugh.

Night cross-country exercises in England were a far cry from the ones we had done in Canada, where city lights could be seen from a consider-able distance. In England we were working in blackout conditions, and if we became lost it was conceivable that ground forces could mistake us for enemy aircraft. Solo navigation was accomplished by pundit crawling. These pundits (beacons) flashed coded letters into the night sky, and if our navigation was right on, we had no difficulty picking them up.

On one occasion a lady officer was giving our class a complete meteor-ology report just prior to one of these night exercises. At the conclusion, she asked if there were any questions. Rip's hand went up. "Will the moon be out?"

Unfortunately, our lady meteorologist saw no humor in the remark and quickly departed without answering. As far as Rip was concerned, how-ever, this was more important than the cloud level.

Rip eventually ended up as an instructor. He was sent to Upavon, the station where King George VI had received his wings many years ear-lier.

One sunny afternoon while we were at Church Lawford, three P-51 Mustangs were rat-racing above the station in the fair-weather cumulus clouds, when two of them collided. Rip Riopelle and I were standing out-side our barracks, and we saw the incident. The third Mustang pilot was desperately "shooting up" (diving low over) our station, trying to draw attention to the accident. We could see only one pilot coming down in a parachute, and we ran toward where he was about to touch down. Before we reached him, he had landed and had walked about 30 feet to a van that had come out from the station. A youngster who had also seen the acci-dent was holding the rip cord, which the pilot had given him before he got into the car. The boy then gave it to me. The next day we found out that the pilot had walked 30 feet on a broken leg before shock had overtaken him. Unfortunately, the other pilot was killed in the crash. Obviously these were three good friends, and their misjudgment would remain forever with the two who had survived.

While at Church Lawford I was assigned with 11 officers to a jury where we witnessed an English court-martial of a sergeant who had gone AWOL. The English wing commander conducting the hearing would determine whether the sergeant was guilty or not, and if so what type of sentencing was due. Our assignment was to listen and decide what we believed the ruling should be, purely as a training assignment.

The sergeant was represented by a civilian lawyer wearing a white, curly wig. We felt this was a little much; nevertheless, that was the way trials were conducted in England. At the trial's conclusion, the wing commander privately asked our opinions, which ranged from "He really hasn't committed that much of a crime" to "He deserves a light prison sentence." We all were amazed when the wing commander told us he would be giving him six months hard labor. So much for English justice.

A somewhat unusual event occurred at the end of our training at Church Lawford. Group Command Headquarters had 16 stations under its jurisdiction. This meant that for testing purposes it would conduct examinations every 16th week at Church Lawford. As luck would have it, our class reached Group Command's 16th week. Ordinarily we would have been tested by the instructors on our station, not by Group Command. There was no notice regarding the subjects we would be tested on until the morning of the examination, which was all verbal. Several nights before Group Command's arrival, I gathered all the members of our hut and spent the evening in the armament section. Using the textbook, I acted as the instructor, asking questions, although I knew no more than the rest of them. After several hours, we packed it in. No one gave me any tutoring.

On the day of the examination, we assembled in a classroom. The testing officer assigned our subjects. "Rip" Riopelle hated navigation, so

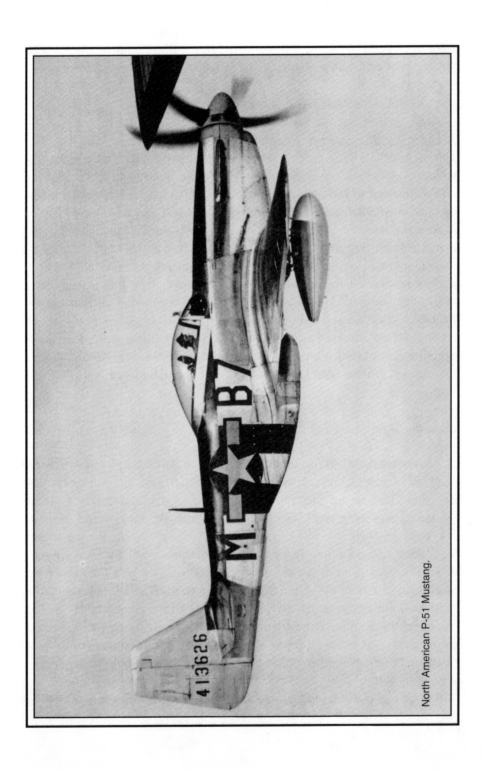

North American P-51 Mustang.

when the officer called out, "Riopelle — navigation," Rip jumped up and yelled, "No, No, not navigation! Give me any other two."

Nevertheless, he got navigation, and he did better than he had anticipated. Would you believe I drew armament? The students who were to be tested for armament had to sit out in the hall until it was their turn to go before the panel. This was somewhat nerve-racking. We would go in one door and leave by another. We were not allowed to talk to the men who had completed their examinations.

I was the last to be tested, and I sat cross-legged on a chair in the middle of the room before a grim group of examiners. I answered their questions, but their expressions gave me no feedback as to whether my responses were correct.

At the conclusion of the questioning the chief instructor, an Englishman, asked me, "Blyth, did you do much 'swatting?'" (the English equivalent of studying).

I answered, "I hope I have done enough."

He then told me that I had received the highest mark in armament they had ever given out, with just one exception, an ex-armament instructor. This rating in armament, together with my experience landing an Oxford under the hood, apparently influenced my selection as the only one in the course to go to Operational Training Unit and then eventually to a squadron. The majority of the students in our course became flying instructors. (On the other hand, perhaps I was the only one who could not qualify to become a flying instructor.)

Chapter 7

Some of Their Stories

*T*IME WEIGHED HEAVILY *on our hands at Stalag Luft 1, so for something to do I kept a log. We were not supposed to do this, but I got hold of a simple writing tablet and started documenting the individual experiences of the members of Room 11, Hut 13. Of the 20 of us in the room, besides Darrell "Atky" Atkinson, Jim Taylor, and me, there were three more "pairs" — crewmen from the same aircraft: Jock Lobban and Mac McKay from Scotland; Spike Holly and P. C. "Smitty" Smith from England; and Bill Cable and Lucien Pidgeon from Canada. The others in our room could not account for*

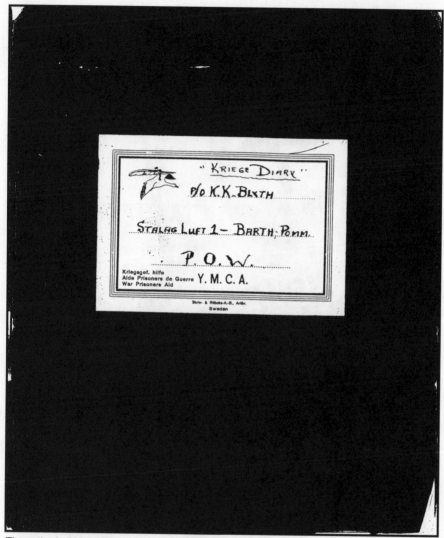

The author's "Kriege Diary" from Stalag Luft 1.

even one other member of their crews. Halifaxes and Lancasters usually had a crew of seven.

Thank goodness, all of my Cradle Crew was safe inside Stalag Luft 1. Though the good Lord had played the major role in this fortunate situation, I felt gratified in having contributed to their safety too. After every mission in earlier days, before we climbed out of our Halifax in the

The RAF's early model Handley Page Halifax, identified by the triangular-shaped fins and rudders, proved to be highly unstable and dangerous for novices to fly at night. This was rectified by the fitting of D-shaped fins and rudders and adjusting the rudder balance so that it could not over-control.

The RCAF's Handley Page Halifax.

The Focke-Wulf 190 was the second-generation German Air Force fighter that gave the Allies a number of headaches as a formidable opponent.

dispersal area, I ran the Cradle Crew through the "abandonment proce-dure," regardless of the hour. This drill was absolutely necessary to ensure that each would know what was expected of him if the aircraft was hit by flak or by enemy fighters, or if it went out of control.

The exercise was boring, mostly because it was simple. The crew could not imagine how they would ever forget it. I wanted the procedure to become automatic, because I was going to be the last one out of the Hali-fax, and I did not want any mistakes that would prevent me from leaving. Reasonable enough? When our aircraft was hit, that is exactly what tran-spired: an automatic abandonment. I was thankful my entire crew was able to bail out safely from our damaged, burning aircraft.

It did not work that way with every bombing crew, however. One of our roommates, Lee Legaarden, from Abernathy, Saskatchewan, was a bom-bardier on a Lancaster. (His pilot had come overseas on the same boat I had come on.) Lee was shot down the same day I was, on the same raid.

Premonitions come to many of us at times, but we rarely heed them. Prior to this mission, Lee had often wondered what would happen if the Lancaster were hit and turned upside down. The escape hatch instead of being on the floor of the aircraft would then be on the top. He knew that an aircraft falling in an inverted position would create intense centrifugal force. There would be no way he could pull himself up to the hatch and bail out of the distressed aircraft. In his mind he formulated a plan if this were ever to happen to him. Unfortunately, it was impossible to test his theory.

Lee's Lancaster was attacked by three Messerschmitt ME-262s, the Germans' best fighter aircraft, a jet with a top speed of 540 mph. Lee's plane was hit almost simultaneously by ground flak. His aircraft caught fire and inverted. His worst nightmare had come true. Would his plan work? No time to think anymore. Do it! Lee was wearing a chest para-chute that he had put on immediately. His wild plan called for him to pull the ripcord INSIDE THE AIRCRAFT! Was he crazy? A small spring-loaded pilot chute came out first, and with his arms around the entire para-chute unit he grabbed this pilot chute and pushed it overhead through the escape hatch. When it caught the slipstream, his skinny frame was sucked out like a cork from a bottle. Lee hit the sides of the aircraft on his exit, resulting in a beautiful shiner, but that was the extent of his injuries. He claimed he was shot at on the way down but the shells pierced only his clothing. He was captured immediately by a German S.S. (storm trooper).

This RAF deHavilland Mark 35 Mosquito, one of the fastest and most versatile light bombers of World War II, is now part of the Confederate Air Force (American Airpower Heritage trust), Midland, Texas.

The deHavilland Mosquito was the wooden wonder — a plywood aircraft that was the fastest operational machine in the air war in Europe for over three years. The version shown here in a postwar photograph is the anti-shipping strike aircraft fitted with rocket launchers. The Mosquito used by the Photographic Reconnaissance Unit of the author's squadron relied on speed as its only defense from enemy fighters.

The skipper, navigator, and mid-upper gunner went down with the aircraft. Lee was unsure what had happened to the rest of the crew.

Jock Lobban and Mac McKay were the navigator and pilot of a twin-engine de Havilland D.H.98 Mosquito. They were with the Photographic Reconnaissance Unit, and their only armament was camera equipment. The PRU photographed potential targets well in advance of a raid. Then immediately after a raid, once the smoke had cleared, they detailed in pictures the extent of the damage. From these pictures our Intelligence could estimate the length of time it would take to put that bombed target back into operation. Lobban and McKay would photograph the damaged area at intervals to determine whether the estimates were accurate and if reconstruction was on schedule. If they were, Bomber Command would have a surprise for the Germans once the job was completed. It had to be demoralizing to find that the rail yards that they had finished restoring over the previous several months had been bombed again the preceding night.

On one of these missions, Lobban and McKay were intercepted by the fast German ME-262s. The Mosquito's top speed was only 450 mph. While trying to escape, Jock and Mac were hit by the German fighter; their rudder was badly damaged, and their starboard engine caught fire. Mac put the Mosquito into a dive; he felt that by going close to the deck he could evade the fighter and at the same time put out the fire. The German MEs followed him down. At a low level the Mosquito was hit again by ground fire from ship defenses.

Jock and Mac were forced to ditch in the water near Albaek, off the coast of Denmark. To their surprise, when they got out of the aircraft the water was only a few feet deep. Their dinghy inflated but they waded to shore. One of the ships that had shot at them was the famous battleship *Lutzow*, the small "pocket battleship" that was later sunk by Group Captain Johnny Fauquier and his 617 Squadron.

Since both Jock and Mac were uninjured, they decided to set out for the Russian lines, but the isthmus they were on was heavily defended, so they were soon captured.

Mac had planned to go on leave after this trip, so he was dressed in 5-A Blues and a "skimmer," his dress hat. For such an easy trip he had not bothered to change into his regular flying suit. Jock was Mac's fifth navigator and Mac was Jock's eleventh pilot. Whoever said the PRU was a piece of cake?

At our briefings, our Intelligence officers had said that if the Germans

This photograph of a Spitfire IX shows why the Spitfire was regarded as probably the most beautiful fighter of the 1939-1945 war.

The early Supermarine Spitfire IX in pre-1942 markings.

A Supermarine Spitfire V of about 1941 shown making a low sweep over a grass airfield in Britain.

had had sufficient petrol supplies they would have had air supremacy within 30 days. However, their low petrol stock limited the amount of time their high-speed jets could remain aloft. They would quickly find their enemy, attack, and head for their base.

General Adolf Galland, the commander of Germany's fighter forces, had wanted only the Focke-Wulf 190 and the Messerschmitt 262 jet fighter to be manufactured. Such a plan was never implemented, however, for in the development stage of the ME-262, the consequences of the 262's high speed on the airframe were unknown. The heat from the Junkers Jumo turbo-jets was greater than anything previously seen in engine development. The nickel and chromium needed for this engine were also in short supply. The Germans went ahead with the project, but were unable to reach the desired production levels. The ME-262 came into use in August 1944; by the end of the war it was in full-scale production.

Room 11 contained virtually every type of air combat participant. Bob

McCracken had flown a Supermarine Spitfire Mark IX; his particular assignment had called for low-level ground strafing. He had attacked and hit a train before he was hit by flak and his aircraft burst into flames, but he was able to push the control stick forward and catapult out. While he was running for ground cover in a clump of woods near Munster, he saw the train he had hit blow up. The woods was a poor choice — he ran smack into Gestapo headquarters.

Bob flew in the same squadron George "Buzz" Beurling, one of Canada's war aces, flew in. Buzz should have been born in another time, for he wanted to fly alone, not under the discipline of a squadron. In combat, fighters had to be able to quickly determine the number of rads of deflection needed to hit an enemy fighter. (A "rad" was the distance from the center to the rim of the fighter's gunsight.) At high speeds he had to calculate the speed of the enemy, and the angle of approach. If the deflection was properly calculated, his cone of fire would hit his target. Bob told me he and another fighter pilot would mathematically work out fighter situations. The calculations would take them some time. Then they would approach Buzz in the mess hall and describe the situation and ask him how much deflection he would "lay on." He would immediately reply, "One and a quarter rads." This would floor Bob McCracken and his buddy, but it was typical of Buzz's skill.

Later on, another friend of mine, Pilot Officer Denis Payne, who flew with the RAF, told me he had met Buzz at an RCAF station in Canada. He was unaware of Buzz's many talents and eagerly accepted a challenge to a game of snooker. Buzz ran the table on him. Afterwards, Buzz asked him if he would like a ride in his single-engine North American Harvard Trainer. Because Denis hadn't flown in some time, he agreed. On takeoff, Buzz did a roll before they had reached 1,000 feet. Denis never went flying with him again. Unfortunately, Buzz wanted to continue flying in combat. After the war he went to Israel where, as a soldier of fortune, he was killed in action.

Smitty — P. C. Smith — and his navigator, Spike Holly, had been flying a twin-engine Bristol Beaufighter when they were shot down on a shipping strike by an FW-190. Spike was wounded in the thigh and right side. They ditched near Norway in a fiord, and both were in the water three hours before they were picked up by the Norwegians. Because Spike was wounded and needed medical attention, the Norwegians felt they had to turn both him and Smitty over to the Germans.

One must remember that Vidkun Quisling, a Norwegian Nazi, was premier of the Norwegian puppet government during the German occupation of Norway in World War II. The word "quisling," meaning anyone who helped betray his country to the enemy — in other words, a traitor — was coined from his name.

Vickers Wellington "Wimpy."

Chapter 8

Training Nearing Completion

*W*E WERE FIRST CREWED UP *at Ossington Operational Training Unit #82 in Nottinghamshire in August 1944. For some unexplainable reason, our crew was complete with the exception of the engineer. We were told we would add one when we reached the conversion unit. As pilot, I now had a navigator, bombardier, wireless operator, mid-upper gunner, and tail gunner. The mid-upper turret on the Wellington had no gunnery equipment, so for practice in the air the tail gunner and mid-upper took turns in the tail turret.*

As a pilot graduated from one aircraft to the next, the first feature he noted was how far he sat from the ground compared to the distance in the previous aircraft he had flown. The second new feature was the number of instruments, which held the pilot in awe until he got used to them. The twin-engine Wellington, affectionately called the "Wimpy," stood some 17 feet from the ground to the pilot's seat.

Some of my most memorable experiences happened while I was in training. Atky, my bombardier, was a washed-out pilot who yearned to take over the controls at any time, as long as I was beside him. From the beginning of my training on the Wellington my crew flew with me. They sat in the belly of the aircraft while my instructor and I did "circuits and bumps " — takeoffs and landings. When it was time for me to fly solo, I had completed six hours and ten minutes dual on the Wellington, and I designated Atky as my copilot. The instructor had Atky do one circuit with him at the controls, and I sat with the rest of the crew in the belly of the aircraft. As soon as we had landed, the instructor climbed out of the aircraft, and I moved back into the pilot position with Atky beside me as the copilot for my first solo in this cigar-shaped aircraft. We had just taken off when I said to Atky, "You've got control."

Our operational aircraft did not provide for a copilot position, but this training aircraft had two sets of steering columns. Atky, almost petrified, grabbed the one in front of him. I had given him no warning I would let him fly the first circuit. With a white-knuckled grip, he made the circuit under my direction. When we turned in for the landing he said, "You're not going to let me land this thing, are you?"

I said, "No way," and took over the controls. He could not wait to find his other bomb-aimer friends and boast about how he had actually flown the very first circuit with the crew, except for the takeoff and the landing.

Atky had a close buddy called Wen Rink, another bombardier, who had been crewed up at Ossington with an experienced pilot. This pilot had already completed his circuit and bumps training, so the crew was able to spend more time on cross-country exercises. This was boring for the pilot, so he often let Wen fly. Wen enjoyed giving Atky a jab about it. But after Atky had made this first circuit, he had the upper hand in their conversations.

Wen bunked three rows over from me. He had an unusual habit. He left his officer hat on until he was fully undressed and pajama clad. It was his last act before hitting the sack. On arising in the morning, the first thing he did was put on that hat and wear it into the washroom. He never talked

The cigar-shaped Vickers Wellington, the standard RAF medium bomber, called the "Wimpy."

about it, but it was another of the unusual habit patterns among aircrew personnel. Superstitious? Hell, no.

On one occasion while practicing circuits and bumps in the Wellington at Ossington, I noticed that each time I made a landing the brake pressure would fall off. When it got dangerously low, I called the tower and explained my problem to the air controllers. They suggested I pull off the runway and face the perimeter track. (All runways in use were reached from the dispersal – where aircraft were kept — via the perimeter track, which encircled the airfield.) They would immediately send out a truck to refill the brake drum.

I was stationary, at right angles to the wind with the two motors barely idling, when I noted a Women's Division corporal riding a bicycle toward me on the perimeter track. From the other direction a small truck was approaching; I assumed it was the one bringing us the brake refill. Unexpectedly the aircraft started to move forward, gathering some speed, and it headed toward several aircraft parked outside a hangar. I could not turn to the right for fear of hitting the girl, and the truck was coming from the left.

I did the only thing that would stop the aircraft: I pulled up the undercarriage. The aircraft collapsed immediately, the propellers breaking into pieces when they touched the ground. Propeller parts flew in all directions. Some of the broken pieces pierced the fuselage outside my station, but fortunately, none came in my direction. A senior officer standing near the hangar saw the incident, and through his intercession I was absolved from any responsibility. He believed I had taken the only practical action. This was another incident of training in an aircraft that was not in first-class condition.

One of the unusual perks we received as officers when we reached the Nottinghamshire Operational Training Unit was that we were awakened each morning by a batwoman (a member of the WAAF – Women's Auxiliary Air Force) with a cup of tea. The English had a lot of expressions that took us some time to get used to. Undoubtedly, the most unusual one was the one our batwoman asked us: "What time do you want to be knocked up in the morning?" I am sure she received a lot of smart remarks that caught her off guard from what was meant to be the simple request: "What time do you wish to be awakened?"

I was not surprised during a navigational cross-country exercise when Atky asked if he could take over the controls. This Wellington had only one control column, so I had to climb out and give my seat to Atky. I had the aircraft well trimmed for straight, level flight, and there appeared to be little danger. The aircraft did not have an automatic pilot, but with it well trimmed, Atky would have little to do sitting at the controls. It gave him a feeling of importance that he was doing the flying.

A small door in the middle of the aircraft prevented the rest of the crew from seeing what was happening up front. Atky was enjoying himself while the gunners in the back were shooting at a drogue target we had trailing on a cable out of the tail. It was then that Atky realized it was his turn to go back to the rear turret and take some gunnery practice. I told him to keep flying and I would take his turn. This appealed to Atky but not to the other crew members when I passed them on my way to the rear turret. They had never had confidence in Atky's flying ability.

When I got to the rear, I plugged in my intercom and called Curly Hughes, the rear gunner, to come out because I was taking Atky's turn. Curly turned whiter than usual when I squeezed by him into the turret. The turret operates somewhat like a motorcycle with a set of handle bars. First, however, the door must close before the turret's guns are operated. Inexperienced as I was, I grabbed the handles and turned them before Curly had shut the doors behind me. I felt I was being sucked out through the open doors. Fortunately I was able to turn the turret back, allowing him to close them. I enjoyed the experience, but the rest of the crew was visualizing what would have happened if I had fallen or had been sucked out of the turret. When I eventually climbed back behind the control column, they felt a great relief. After we landed Curly said, "I hope you will never do that again. When we took off, I was 18 years old. I am now 21."

Atky always seemed to be a trial for the crew in one way or another. During virtually every mission over Germany, on the return trip it was necessary for him to use the john in the central part of the aircraft. For this venture he had to take a portable oxygen bottle with him. Although the aircraft was usually cold, it certainly was not "air-conditioned." After he had stunk up the aircraft one too many times and was about to do it again I asked Brock, our mid-upper gunner, while Atky was making his way to the "crapper," to let me know when he was poised over the can. Brock could see Atky from his location in the turret, and when I got Brock's signal, I put the aircraft into a corkscrew evasive procedure. When Atky had righted himself I apologized and said that I must have hit an air pocket. We continued to hit air pockets until he finally got the message and paced himself better.

Fortunately, our crew became "family" and went everywhere together. Atky and I bought a small car which we named "the Flea." When we were on leave we would set out for the town of Thirsk to catch a train, with all seven of us jammed into the car. This meant double-decking those in the back seat. Admittedly it was not too comfortable for the ones on the bottom or at the side of the car. With that kind of load, the tires would rub against the body, and the frame would become hot. We unloaded in the town square, amazing many of the town locals when seven of us climbed out of such a small car. It looked like a circus routine!

We had bought the Flea for £50 — around $250 in U.S. dollars at that time — and we enjoyed having our own transportation. However, from the very first day we bought the car, it caused us problems. Before its actual purchase, Atky and I test drove it into Newark-on-Trent. I was wearing my uniform, but I had a pair of slippers on my feet; I was not expecting to get out of the car. In the center of town the Austin stopped and would not start up again. Because neither of us had any great mechanical experience, we were baffled. Lifting the hood, we could see gas in the small gas tank, yet the car would not move. Several bobbies — English policemen — wandered over to see what our problem was. They looked at the gas tank too (fortunately we were using regular petrol and not aircraft petrol, which was illegal), and finally one of them told us to pull the small stopper beside the tank to correct our problem. Apparently this car had no fuel gauge, so we drove it until it stopped. Then we would pull the stopper, and we had one gallon of petrol remaining. Because we could travel 40 or 50 miles on a gallon of gasoline, this was no great problem.

Mac McQuarrie, a used car salesman before enlisting and coming overseas, had sold us the car. Soon other aircrew had McQuarrie get them a car. We nicknamed him "Turnover McQuarrie," for he developed a great side business in used cars.

During the entire time we owned the car, we never had to use the few gasoline ration coupons that had come with the car's purchase. One day I set out on my own to find a gas station where I could make a deal for gasoline. I found a place where I could get gas by trading my clothing coupons. I rarely needed these because my family sent me the few extra things I needed from time to time. Neither Atky nor anyone else knew where I did my negotiating.

There were very few private autos on the roads during the war, so naturally the police were suspicious when they saw one. One time Atky and I were alone on the highway. A police car spotted us and pulled us over. This time we had the wrong kind of petrol in the tank. The officer asked us whether we had our insurance certificate, which fortunately we had in the glove compartment. We were unaware that it had to be displayed on the dashboard. We were warned that if we did not have one, we would be

Atky and the author doing a minor repair job on the "Flea."

fined $50. It surprised us that he had mentioned the fine in dollars, not pounds.

"You lads 'ave an 'in' with the adjudant?" (Apparently an indirect query as to where we were getting our petrol supplies.) I flashed the few gasoline coupons I carried, and that deterred him from looking into the gas tank — a really close call.

On another occasion, a buddy of mine, who worked out in the gymnasium and fashioned himself quite a boxer, entered an assault-at-arms competition at another air station some 30 miles away. He was courting a young WAAF who talked Atky and me into driving her over to the tournament. We set out after dark in a snowstorm, which made it difficult to see where we were going. The only light we drove by came from slits in the headlamps on the car. Fortunately, I had good night vision.

I had not had an opportunity to go to my friendly petrol station to fill up before we left, but I believed we could make it back with what we had. However, the air station was farther than we had thought, and I became concerned that we might run out of petrol on the way back. Our WAAF friend told us not to worry, because she had a friend in the Hospital Motor Corps who would undoubtedly help us. The "help" amounted to telling us which trucks had a supply tank we could tap to get some gas. She provided us with an empty can, and I began siphoning this valuable petrol, which was making what I thought was a helluva racket landing in the can. I thought it could be heard for miles in the stillness of the night. All of a sudden a window was thrown open, and a loud male voice shouted, "What the hell's going on out there?"

We decided not to reply and yanked the tube from the tank and quickly departed. We felt sure we would be held up at the front gate, but we managed to get through without any problem. After we were some ten miles down the road, we felt safe enough to stop and transfer the petrol from the can to the gas tank. (By the way, our buddy got beat in the boxing match.)

During our training at the Nottinghamshire Operational Training Unit, we had our first experience with the early stages of radar, called "Gee." Gee operated on a signal sent out from ground stations which was picked up on a screen inside the aircraft by the navigator and bombardier. From this signal they could plot our location. We had to practice "homing exercises" in the air with this equipment. On one particular day we had been practicing for some time. We were satisfied with our efforts and were about to return to base when Jim Taylor, our navigator, decided to show off and impress me with the effectiveness of Gee. We were at 10,000 feet over the town of Newark-on-Trent. Jim bet me that he could "home" in on the swimming pool in Newark and let me know when he was dead center over it. I thought that this was a reasonable bet, primarily because I could see the pool and would know for sure whether he had made it. The bet involved the loser buying a drink for all the crew. We were dead center over the pool when he shouted, "Now!"

I thought, "What a piece of equipment!" After we got back to the station and everyone was having a drink on my tab, they could not keep to themselves how they had pulled one over on me. I was unaware that Brock, the mid-upper gunner, standing in an open turret could see the ground and the pool. He had given Jim hand signals. Rotten pool I called it, but they had downed their drinks by that time.

At the end of our training on the Wellington we had to do a night cross-country flight from Ossington down to the south of England. Our route took us along the coast and then up to Bristol, our target. Instead of carrying bombs we had an infra-red camera in the bomb bay. We were to proceed as if we were on a bombing mission, making our run to the target and opening the bomb doors at precisely the time we were to drop the bombs. The bombing tit would be pressed, and the infra-red camera would take a picture of the target. The target was invisible to the naked eye, so we could not determine our success or failure until we returned to our base and developed the film to see whether we had made a hit. In order to control the operation, the target was open for only a few minutes. Planes that were early or late returned with no picture.

Ordinarily this would have been an easy exercise, but something always seemed to happen to make it a little more interesting. At the briefing, our crew had been informed that the wind speed would be in the neighborhood of 45 mph. As we neared the turn from the coast and headed toward the target, the navigator was getting a double Gee image, resulting in two different wind speeds — one in the 45 mph range and the other around 100 mph. He had Adam "Wat" Watson, the wireless operator, take some ground fixes, taking some more valuable time. All ground stations emitted a signal that the wireless operator could pick up on his radio equipment. By recording several of these signals he could plot them; where the signals crossed was our exact location. This was an excellent system for cross-checking radar equipment for accuracy.

The crew panicked somewhat about the short time that the target would be open. An incorrect wind speed would assure failure. However, the radio fix Wat provided validated that 100 mph was the correct wind speed. With this additional information we were able to hit the target on time.

We thought this was a big deal. The exercise, called a Bullseye, was effective in developing for each crew the stringent conditions under which they would fly in operations. When we were on missions, we were expected to bomb the target within 30 seconds of the time assigned to us.

While in training at Ossington, we were introduced to a pressure bell, used to demonstrate to aircrew members the effects of the lack of oxygen. By adjusting the pressure, oxygen conditions at various altitudes could be simulated. We entered the bell and sat down. The doctor in charge remained outside, but he could see the activity inside. He gave us certain instructions.

At the outset we were not wearing oxygen masks, and the doctor reproduced inside the bell the oxygen level at 15,000 feet. Then he directed our attention to our fingernails, which had turned blue. We were in no immediate danger at this level. He asked Wat if he would be the guinea pig for the balance of the experiment. When Wat agreed, the doctor told the rest of the crew to put on oxygen masks. After we had "climbed" to 20,000 feet the doctor asked Wat, "Are you able to send a MTB?" (message to base).

"Yes sir," he replied.

The doctor asked him to start counting backwards by odd numbers beginning with 100. He started, "99, 97, 95, 46, 37, 65." He was getting a bit woozy.

We were at "25,000 feet" when the doctor asked Wat, "Can you still send a MTB?"

"Yep."

His eyes were starting to shut, and his head was beginning to flop. There were playing cards on the table, and the doctor asked Wat to count them. He did his best, but he was almost out by this time. Then the doctor asked me to remove Wat's wristwatch in full view of Wat and the rest of the crew. Wat offered no resistance.

The doctor told me to connect Wat's oxygen mask. Wat immediately became alert.

"Can you send a MTB?"

"Absolutely." He had totally recovered.

"What time is it?" the doctor asked.

Wat looked at his wrist and not seeing his watch, said, "I must have left it in my other clothes." He was absolutely unaware that I had removed it from him. He said he had had no feeling of passing out, but was oblivious to what had happened. We learned a good lesson, and we all remembered the importance of oxygen in our non-pressurized aircraft.

We never participated in a Nickel Raid — a leaflet drop over territory (such as France or Belgium) that had been overrun by the Germans. It may be that in December 1944 this raid had been discarded as a training exercise. Many of the earlier crews during their final training had been part of such a program. The experience was considered extremely practical because it simulated an actual bombing raid. There was a strong possibility that the aircraft could be attacked by fighters or hit by ground flak.

After completing the Operational Training Unit, the crew went on a 12-day leave. Then on October 11, we were posted to Dalton, where we added an engineer to our crew. Because we were very young there was concern at first that Doug Grey, an old guy of 26, might not mix well with us. After all, he was the only married crew member, and he had five children.

Nothing could have been farther from the truth. From the start we nicknamed him "Pop," and he became our senior citizen. (The crew decided to call me "Baldy," because when my hair was wet it was so thin that it appeared I was bald.) At Dalton, Doug and I spent long hours of study on engine handling. It would be a big move from a twin-engine to a four-engine aircraft, so we worked hard on our studies. Doug quickly showed us that he was a great selection for our flight engineer. We were fortunate to find another member who not only blended in with the crew but was efficient and knew his trade well. It was up to Doug to make sure all the engines were working properly and that the aircraft was developing maximum fuel utilization.

On November 8, 1944, we were temporarily transferred to Topcliffe, and finally, on November 29, we were posted to Dishforth #1664 Conversion Unit. The crew made the 15-minute flight in a Halifax III. Atky and I drove the Flea to Dishforth — an interesting trip. Because Atky was lousy behind the wheel, usually the driving was left to me. There was a small mountain range en route, and the Flea just did not have enough power to get us to the top. It petered out. Atky wondered what we were going to do. I declared, "We're just going to sit here until an American Army convoy comes by, and they'll have a rope and tow us to the summit."

"You're nuts."

Would you believe that in less than an hour an American convoy did come by, and the last truck had a rope in it. They gladly towed us to the top of the mountain. Atky could not believe it. He said I was just lucky. I told him he had to have faith.

Our first close-up look at the Halifax bomber was awesome. To me the Halifax looked immense after flying the much smaller Wellington. Its four Hercules radial engines and overall size looked overwhelming. Comparing it to today's sleek jet-propelled Air Force equipment would be ludicrous.

It was Shakespeare who appropriately said, "Oh, to be in England now that April's here," but he never wrote about the fall and winter. The weather conditions during these seasons determined how long it would take to complete our training, which called for ten days of ground school and ten days of flying. Weather conditions required that we stay at Dishforth for six weeks.

We learned that when an operational aircraft became unserviceable it was usually sent to a Conversion Unit, where some unsuspecting greenhorn pilot would train with it. Many times our training exercise was "washed out" because the equipment was unsatisfactory for flying. In fact, during the night I had to solo on takeoffs and landings, the aircraft in service was backfiring and scaring the bejeepers out of me. The instructor, however, did not appear to be too disturbed by this. He asked, "Do you want to go solo?"

Like a dummy I replied, "Naturally."

After we dropped off our instructor, Doug Grey joined me up front as we taxied out to the runway. Atky and Doug shared the copilot responsibilities. On this exercise I had asked Doug to be copilot because I was not happy with the way the engines were performing, and I could not allow the rest of the crew to know my concern. To add to our troubles, it was raining again. The combination of wet weather and a questionable aircraft did not sit well with me. During my dual instruction the crew was seated in the center of the aircraft, unaware of what I was experiencing. They were no doubt thinking, "Here we go on another circuit."

We started down the runway. At about the point where any choice of stopping had passed, the starboard outer engine backfired and shut off immediately. You can land on three engines, but definitely cannot take off on three. I grabbed the dead throttle and pushed it forward, hoping it would refire with the other three. What a relief Doug and I felt when it refired and we were able to take off, complete the circuit, and land. Only Doug, who was standing beside me, knew what a close call we had just had. I would definitely not make another circuit in this aircraft.

My crew and I climbed out and reported that the aircraft should be taken out of service. Other pilots told me of similar experiences they had had with equipment that should never have been used for flight training. While most of the aircraft at the training units worked efficiently, too many were not up to the standard we felt they should be.

On another occasion we had to call off one of our night bombing exercises because the heavy, low clouds made it impossible for the bombardier to see the target. We decided to return to our base, and we prepared to land. I checked the brake pressure by squeezing the brake lever, which is part of the steering column, and checking the gauge. Everything appeared to be in good working order when I landed the aircraft on the runway, but when I attempted to apply the brakes nothing happened. I tried again and still nothing. I was going hell-bent for election, and fast running out of runway. What immediately came to my mind was that between the end of the runway and the dispersal was the Great North Road. Mentally, I could visualize some poor driver moseying along and our running smack dab into him. I had no more time to think about a potential tragedy. I had to do something and it had better be fast! We still carried our full load of practice bombs, and although they should not detonate if I pulled up the undercarriage, I was, nevertheless, afraid that sliding on our belly on the concrete runway would cause them to dislodge and explode. I had one other option.

There was nothing to my right but open space, so I gently opened the port outer engine. The aircraft slowly turned to the open area. It had rained, and the ground was very soft. As soon as we left the runway and hit the soft ground the undercarriage buckled, and we dropped flat on our belly. The metal blades of the propellers dug deep into the ground. I did not have to tell the crew to get out. They were out before I knew it.

Group Command Headquarters said I took the wrong corrective action. They believed that I should have pulled up the undercarriage while still on the runway. They grounded me for ten days. What they did not know was that at the end of the runway, before one reached the Great North Road, there were ten-foot-high mounds of gravel for road work. If I had pulled up the undercarriage as they prescribed, I would have slid into these gravel piles and no doubt would not have been around to tell about it. I had made a choice. It had to be quick. If I was right I would walk away — wrong and I would be a goner. We walked away. 'Nuff said.

Weather conditions at Dishforth were making us irritable, and the Nissen huts we lived in were damp. The small coal fire did not last through the night. One of us would have to get up and restoke it before the others in the hut would climb out of the sack. These huts, the bane of all Canadian aircrew, were named after the inventor, Lord Nissen. They were somewhat simple structures on concrete pads, with curved metal pieces forming the walls and ceiling. There were six cots on each side of the hut, with a walkway in the middle. The walkway was the only area in which one could stand erect. The beds were always cold and damp. Throughout our six-week stay, none of us ever got warm.

Our final cross-country exercise was programmed from Dishforth, in central England, to a point in Scotland and then across the Irish Sea to a point just off the coast of Ireland. We would continue across the Irish Sea back to Brighton in southern England and finally return to our station. Inclement weather had delayed this exercise twice before. During this particular flight we had hardly reached our programmed altitude of 15,000 feet when Doug reported that we had a hot starboard engine and needed to feather it. Feathering not only stopped the engine, it turned the propeller blades so that they created no wind resistance. I told Jim Taylor we could not hold 15,000 feet on three engines and would have to fly the entire exercise at 10,000 feet. This we decided to do. Doug and I constantly watched the other three engines' temperatures, and planned where we would land or ditch if another engine heated up. Fortunately nothing happened, and we logged up another wild one. I must admit that the crew was not too happy with their skipper, and this was a nervous flight for all of them; but Atky boasted about our prowess to the Chief Flying Officer, who thought we were out of our minds for not aborting the exercise.

It was always a possibility that land-based aircraft that had been shot up or had experienced engine malfunction would have to land on water — ditch — something to avoid if at all possible. Thus, an exercise was devised at the Conversion Unit to give us some training on what we should do. An abandoned Halifax was set up on blocks or stilts with every control wired to a panel inside another room. At the beginning of the exercise all the panel lights would be on. When we went through the ditching procedure, our actions would turn off the lights. Every member of the crew had a specific assignment. When we believed we had completed what was necessary for the ditching, we climbed out to check the lighted panel. If any lights were still on, it was apparent who had slipped up. It was a good drill, and fortunately we never had to employ it. In actual practice, a dinghy would be inflated when the aircraft had settled on the water; hopefully everyone could climb aboard and quickly leave the area before the aircraft sank.

The day finally came in mid-January 1945 when we got our posting to 408 Squadron stationed at the town of Linton, in Yorkshire, England, on the river Ouse — Linton-on-Ouse. I had to do several cross-country and bombing exercises before I made my first trip over enemy territory. Bomber Command instructions called for the pilot to make one "second dickie" trip before he could take his crew on a daylight raid and two "second dickie" trips before he could take them on a night mission.

We were eager to get about the business for which we had been trained. I was informed that the training program for a pilot up to this point cost about $50,000. After completing my first mission, this value would rise to $100,000.

The experience of a completed raid was invaluable to a new pilot. When an experienced crew carrying a second dickie was lost, the Allies lost a professional flight team, but also the new crew on the station became a "headless crew." Rarely was it possible to find a single pilot to take over this crew. Superstition crept in. Both the headless crew and the pilot wondered whether they had been assigned to a jinxed crew.

The Junkers Ju88 was a mainstay of the Luftwaffe for most of World War II. This particular aircraft is at the USAF Museum at Dayton, Ohio.

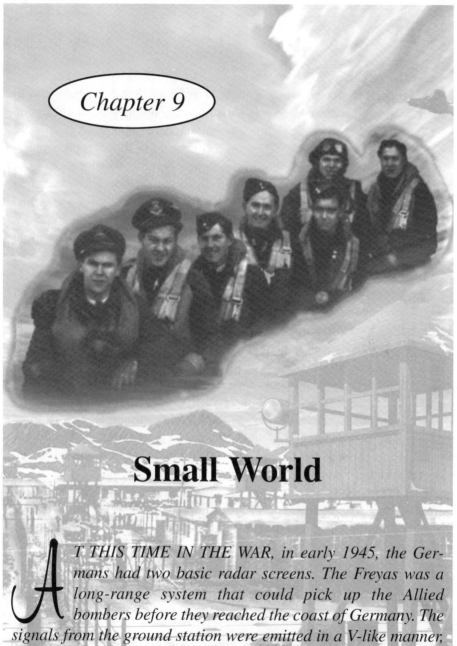

Chapter 9

Small World

AT THIS TIME IN THE WAR, in early 1945, the Germans had two basic radar screens. The Freyas was a long-range system that could pick up the Allied bombers before they reached the coast of Germany. The signals from the ground station were emitted in a V-like manner, producing a radar network that gave the Freyas operators the ability to identify the early bomber penetration once the bomber stream broke through the radar screen. The Allied forces were aware of this capability and on bombing missions usually maintained a low altitude as long as possible. In our case, we flew under the screen at 2,000 feet until we crossed the coast, then immediately climbed to our bombing altitude. The Giant Wurzburg radar equipment was more accurate and was used once the bombers were picked up on the Freyas to direct the fighters to the area under attack.

One of the techniques used by the German night fighters, particularly the Junkers Ju88 twin-engine medium fighter bomber, was for them to be "homed" by their Giant Wurzburg ground station towards the bombing stream. As the fighters came into range, they would pick out one Allied bomber on the radar screen in their aircraft and zero in on it from below. When they were close enough to make visual identification, the night fighter would fly under the belly of the aircraft, usually out of sight of the bomber's gunners, and strafe it with upward-firing guns, blowing a hole in the underside of the bomber.

As navigator of a Lancaster, Bill Neilson, an Englishman from Cheshire, was involved in just such an incident. Only he and three other members of the seven-man crew were able to bail out. He went out through the hole in the bottom of the aircraft. They were an experienced crew; the tail gunner had shot down two aircraft and had another "probable." Yet, in spite of their skill, the Junkers 88 had crept up on them unnoticed. Bill had managed to evade the German ground forces for three days before being captured — quite an undertaking, because he had been wounded in the leg. He limped through a railway station without being recognized, but he was caught trying to steal a bike.

D. J. "Tommy" Thomas, from South Wales, had had a similar experience. He was a bombardier on a Lancaster who met his Waterloo while on a night mission. Once again, the gunners did not see the Junkers 88 approach from below. The Lancaster was hit in the bomb bay, but Tommy was able to get out before the bombs exploded. He was the only one able to do so. He spoke a little German, which helped him elude the enemy for four days, but he was eventually captured by civilians and turned over to the military.

The only member in our room who had flown a Stirling bomber was Jack Caldwell, a bombardier from New South Wales, Australia. The Stirling was a first-line four-engine heavy bomber that, unfortunately, with its shorter wingspan was unable to operate effectively above 15,000 feet. Because Lancasters and Halifaxes were able to operate from 22,000 to 25,000 feet, the Stirlings found themselves assigned to dropping supplies and picking up and dropping our agents behind enemy lines, by no

The Short Stirling was the first of the new four-engine heavy bombers ordered in 1936 and beginning to enter the RAF in 1941. The Stirling was excellent in the air, carrying a full bomb load in a fuselage-length bomb bay, but it was tricky on the ground because with the tail down, the wings blanketed the fin and rudder.

means a piece of cake. It required almost exclusively night penetrations below 500 feet and taking off and landing on makeshift runways. It also required exacting navigation and landing with very little ground identification.

Jack's aircraft was shot down while he was on a supply mission to Norway. Again, the Junkers 88 night fighter was the villain. The Stirling's gunners spotted the night fighter before they were hit and warned the pilot, who started an evasive maneuver known as a corkscrew, a diving and spiraling motion in the direction of the attack, followed by an upward-spiraling action. If executed at the right moment, this twisting action by the bomber made it difficult for the fighter to get a good bead on the aircraft without blacking out in the process. In this particular instance, it is conceivable the corkscrew was started too soon and the fighter was able to stay on the bomber's tail and make a hit. Only Jack and three of the crew were able to bail out. He landed on the island of Hees and was soon captured near an army barracks. As he floated down in his parachute, he saw his aircraft explode nearby.

Usually 30 bombing missions constituted a tour. Because the pilots made one or two flights as second dickies before taking their crew on a mission, the balance of the crew would have 28 or 29 trips when the tour was completed.

Whether or not they liked to admit it, most crew members were superstitious. Sometimes they carried personal mementos, such as special pieces of clothing, or they had special routines that they never varied. They hated to have a substitute crew member when a regular got sick. Crew members believed disaster would surely befall them if they varied their routines or had a new member in their crew. Night missions were considered more dangerous than daylight runs. When their pilot had completed his 29th mission they would ask that number 30 be a daylight mission. A daylight mission was usually considered a "piece of cake."

Bill Cable, from Winnipeg, Manitoba, had to be excited that they were able to have their "Number 30" for their pilot as a daylight, the target being the prefabricated submarine base at Hamburg, Germany. This was the same raid on which we "bought it." Cable was the bombardier on a Hally (Halifax). The kite was hit in the bomb bay by flak, but the bombs did not explode. Almost simultaneously the aircraft was attacked by three ME-262s. (I wonder if it was the same threesome that came after us.) All the crew bailed out, but the pilot died later from the wounds he received before leaving the aircraft. I often wondered when Bill returned to England whether the squadron gave him credit for a full tour.

The wireless gunner on the same aircraft was Lucien Pidgeon, called "Pidge" for short. The third man out of the aircraft, he was uninjured. He landed near an army camp and was captured almost immediately. Pidge was quite a colorful character — a great kidder. Although a French-Canadian from Montreal, Quebec, he spoke English very well. However, his pronunciation of some words would get a rise out of us. I recall one night when he awoke and yelled, "I forgot to take my en-ER-gy pill." He had to climb out of his third-tier bunk to take one. He believed that if he did not take these every day something bad would happen to him. It was not too long before everyone in the hut referred to them as "enERgy" pills. The pills were the Horlick tablets we received in our Red Cross parcels — in today's lingo, "vitamin pills."

Pidge always called me "Kennet." Maybe "Kenneth" is hard for a French-Canadian to say. Whether by design or corruption of the name, he called Bill "Sable" instead of Cable, and another nickname was quickly born, which Bill bore throughout his stay in the camp.

The other Montrealer in the room was Roger Savard. Like Smitty, he had also been the pilot of a Beaufighter who met his match while on a shipping strike to Norway. Roger was hit almost simultaneously by ground flak and an FW-190. He crashed on the ice, and the navigator went "in" with the kite. Roger was picked up by Norwegians and later turned over to the Germans.

Rex Ebert, an Australian, had been a navigator-bomber on a Bristol Beaufighter (anti-shipping torpedo bomber). He was the only one in the room who had not been shot down. On a moonlit night he and his pilot were flying over the water at deck level. The pilot misjudged their height, and they plowed into the deck. The pilot was killed, but Rex was able to escape in an inflatable dinghy. The dinghy had a small puncture, but Rex managed to remain afloat long enough to be picked up by a Norwegian fishing boat. He clearly remembered that the Norwegians turned him over to the Germans at 3:00 a.m. the night he crashed.

I was never aware of how many missions constituted a tour for fighter pilots and their crews. It had to be considerably more than the 30 required for bomber crews. Bombing missions were never under 6 hours, and the longest one for our crew was 9 hours and 18 minutes. Fighter missions, on the other hand, were usually quite short, varying according to the type of mission.

Bob McCall had been a fighter pilot of a Beaufighter. He was shot down by ground flak off Bergen while on a shipping strike. These strikes were particularly dangerous because they had two extremely deadly enemies to cope with — the enemy fighter aircraft and the very accurate ground flak. At low level the ground flak was more concentrated than the high-level flak. The crew was able to successfully evade an FW-190 that attacked, but the land flak was another matter. After being hit, McCall and his navigator were forced to ditch just off the coast. They, too, were picked up by a Norwegian fishing boat, which was escorted by a German fishing boat. Both the pilot and the navigator were OK. This was another "last trip" that didn't pan out. It was trip number 52, which would have completed their tour.

Altogether, six members of Room 11 had been picked up by the Nor-

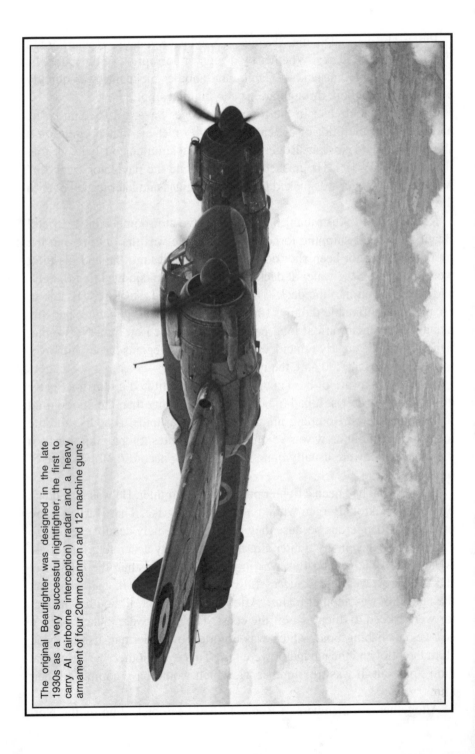

The original Beaufighter was designed in the late 1930s as a very successful nightfighter, the first to carry AI (airborne interception) radar and a heavy armament of four 20mm cannon and 12 machine guns.

The Bristol Beaufighter had a number of variants. Above is the anti-shipping Mark X fitted with rocket launchers and capable of carrying a torpedo.

The Hawker Typhoon was a second-generation fighter that proved most effective in the ground-attack role and low-level operations from 1943 onward.

wegians and eventually released to the Germans. Evidently, Norwegian Nazi Vidkun Quisling's puppet government had instilled fear in the heart of every Norwegian.

Room 11 had an unusual mixture of bombing crews, fighter aircraft crews that had engaged in fighter activity, and fighter aircraft crews that had dropped land mines onto German shipping lanes. Jeff Kinsey, an Englishman, was the only pilot in our room who had flown a Hawker Typhoon, a single-seat ground-attack aircraft with a maximum speed of 416 mph. His misfortunes had come about while he was supporting a raid on the Rhine Bridgehead. Due to his low-level attack, the ground flak became Kinsey's undoing. His engine took the hit, and Jeff crashed one mile from the front. He was immediately surrounded by German paratroopers and taken captive. Before he was hit, he had scored on one tank and two or three trucks; all were destroyed.

If there is one story about the members of my room that was more amazing than the others, it had to be Moon Mullen's. Moon was a Spitfire pilot from New Brunswick, one of Canada's maritime provinces. While flying on patrol with the City of Oshawa squadron near Osnabrück, in central northwest Germany, the squadron noticed a lone P-51 Mustang flying in the vicinity of its patrol. Since it was a friendly American aircraft, Mullen and the rest of the squadron had no reason to be concerned by its appearance. Suddenly the Mustang fired on the patrol from a considerable distance, hitting Moon. Moon bailed out, landed in an anti-aircraft post, and was captured immediately by the Germans. The Spitfire bore a slight resemblance to the FW-190, but the pilot of the Mustang must have had poor aircraft recognition. He must have thought he would go down in the record books if he knocked down a covey of FW-190s. Moon never found out what happened to the Mustang pilot, but Moon was determined to file charges when he got back to his base. The other pilot faced possible court-martial.

A postscript to this story occurred after the war had ended. My wife and I were visiting a friend in Montreal who had been a Spitfire pilot. He had invited another buddy and his wife to join us for dinner. My friend, Don Gray, a culinary master, had prepared the roast and fixings and was busy in the kitchen. In the living room, the "hangar doors" were open as Gray's buddy and I talked of our war experiences. I had to tell him the story of Moon Mullen's having been shot down by a Mustang. When Don came

This North American P-51 Mustang I, with Allison engine, was used for ground attack, especially against trains in France.

back from the kitchen to join the conversation, he said, "We had a guy in our squadron who was shot down by a Mustang."

Surprised, I looked at him and asked, "Was his name Moon Mullen?"

"Yes," Don answered, "but how the hell did you know?"

Can you imagine? My good buddy from Montreal was in the same squadron and on the same patrol! Small world.

Chapter 10

The 408 Squadron

*D*URING THE LATTER PART OF 1942, the Royal *Canadian Air Force Six Group had been formed. Prior to that date, Canadian airmen were intermingled with Royal Air Force personnel; they had no individual identification as a group. Six Group grew rapidly, and I was for-tunate to be based at one of its stations with 408 Squadron.*

The 408 Squadron was located at Linton-on-Ouse, Yorkshire. A simple orientation would be to say it was located in central England. The Ouse was a narrow river — not very majestic as rivers go — but it ran through beautiful English countryside and emptied into the North Sea. 408 Squadron shared this facility with the 426 Thunderbird Squadron.

The 408 was also known as the Goose Squadron, the goose being the centerpiece of our logo. The name originated from Kingsville, Ontario, where Jack Miner had made famous his Canadian goose sanctuary. Miner had developed the sanctuary over a period of four years. It had taken that long before the geese would identify this location as a feeding stop. Miner was anxious to learn as much as possible about the migratory flight of these birds, so he captured the birds at the sanctuary and placed a band on one of their legs before releasing them. In this manner he was able to chart their migratory flight. It was an appropriate logo for our squadron.

In January 1945, squadron life with 408 was very relaxed — that is, until a mission was called by Six Group Headquarters. Basically we had two sets of orders — stand down and standby. When the weather was "beastly," as the English liked to describe bad weather over England, and was over the potential target areas, we were on stand down. Dances were arranged in the mess. Some of the men went into town and had a great time in the pubs. In general, we all kicked up our heels. But once the standby order came, we quickly settled down to business.

I recall one night when we were on stand down and a party was going full swing in the mess. Suddenly out of the blue we got a standby order, which killed the party immediately. We were told to hit the sack, for we would have only a few hours' sleep before briefing. There were a few big heads at briefing the next morning, and some of the guys had trouble recovering. Many a crew when it took off did so with the pilot or some other crew member half in the bag. Most of the time, and this time in particular, the crew was skillful enough to handle the mission without causing a disaster. The difficulty, of course, with the stand down and standby orders was that the crews could not predict when the change would be called. We certainly did not operate on a nine-to-five schedule.

The British and Canadian forces usually referred to raids as "sorties." The American forces called them "missions." It was some time before I found out that "sortie" was the French word for "exit." After that, I preferred to call them "raids" or "missions." Too many Canadian crews had "exited" for my liking.

When a raid was called, the navigators and bombardiers were first ordered into the briefing room, usually an hour before the rest of the crew. This gave them time to prepare their charts so that they could give their undivided attention to the general briefing when it commenced. Once they were in the briefing room, they were not permitted to leave until the entire briefing was completed. No one attended the briefing who was not going on the mission except the squadron commander. The squadron commander flew about three missions per month; otherwise, Group Headquarters would have been changing squadron commanders too frequently. During my stay, Wing Commander Freddy Sharpe was squadron commander of 408 Squadron.

Whenever I think of Freddy Sharpe I am reminded of an experience he had on one of his missions. On one particular night raid Freddy and his crew were starting the bombing run, and Freddy was responding to the "left, left, steady" directions, which he thought were coming from his bombardier, when all of a sudden his bombardier shouted at him, "What the hell are you doing?"

"I'm doing what you are telling me."

"Up to now I haven't said a damn thing."

Would you believe his aircraft was close enough to another one that somehow his headset was picking up the instructions of a bombardier in another aircraft — just another of the many weird experiences that seemed to happen to aircrew.

In 1968, Canada integrated the Navy, Army, and Air Force, and before his death, in 1991, Freddy Sharpe was General, Chief of the Defense Staff of Canada's entire military establishment.

But back to the briefings of 408 Squadron — they were always exciting and well organized. Every one opened in the same manner: "The target for tonight is . . . ."

Simultaneously all eyes would become riveted on the target map. When airmen noted the mission was to the Ruhr Valley, they got lumps in their throats. The Ruhr Valley was the most heavily defended area in all Germany, second only to Berlin. In Happy Valley — as it was called by the crews — there was more flak and more enemy fighter activity than on any other target, causing tension that never abated.

We were first given a detailed description of the target and the area around it, and of the purpose of the mission. We were warned about where to expect enemy aircraft and enemy flak. Weather information – both local and what we might encounter en route — was very detailed. Anticipated climatic conditions in the target area and possible target visibility for bombing was described — or we were told if we would be sighting on flares. The time of the raid was given only once; after that, all references to it were plus or minus H-hour. Each crew was assigned its height over the target.

Absolute quiet reigned in the briefing room, except for clarification questions. The success of the mission and the lives of crew members could depend on everyone fully understanding his role in the operation.

New crews on the squadron were given one of the surplus aircraft, usually a different aircraft for every mission. Eventually they had assigned aircraft. Our crew was proud of *E.Q.-J.* The phonetic name for *J* is "Jig," which did not appeal to us, so we changed it to *J* for "Johnny." The station fought us for a while on this, but eventually gave in. The station name for communication purposes was Dogbark. The squadron name was Bargeman. On return from a mission my call to the station would be: "Bargeman *Johnny* to Dogbark."

And the station air controller would reply, "This is Dogbark; come in Bargeman *Johnny*."

Our next project was to let everyone know this was our aircraft. Because the average age of the crew at this time was only a little over 18, we were referred to as the "Cradle Crew." We decided to adopt this as our insignia. On the nose of *J-Johnny* I drew a giant stork wearing a top hat. Instead of a stork holding a baby in a diaper, I drew in a bomb.

We made a raid in *Johnny* before I had completed my artwork; I had only outlined the insignia in chalk. When we were turning on the runway for the takeoff, our padre, Mac McLeod, was there along with many of the station personnel ready to give us the thumbs up signal for a safe trip. Later I was told he had asked what the outline depicted. After being told, he said: "I hope it isn't open season for storks wherever they're going."

Somehow all the station personnel knew when a mission was on. They would find their way to the runway in use and, in unison, give us the thumbs up sign as we lined up for takeoff. All the pilots acknowledged this emotional salute by giving them a thumbs up in return. The green light flashed from the control caravan, and we were on our way. We raced down the runway, and the engines roared as they reached full throttle. Only the engineer and I were up front; the balance of the crew was seated in the middle of the aircraft. The excitement always built as the motors roared waiting for the tail to rise. The pilot could feel that slight motion, and shortly the aircraft would lift off and the mission was on. There was

always concern when we had to use the short runways that we might run
out of runway before we had enough speed for takeoff.

After our arrival at Linton and 408 Squadron, the first two trips called
by Bomber Command were night raids to Mainz and Wanne-Eickel, in the
heart of the Ruhr Valley. Only 86 aircraft from Six Group participated in
the Mainz raid, and all returned safely. On the trip to Mainz, I was copilot
(actually "second dickie") to Flying Officer Dean and his crew. The Halifax used on operations did not have dual controls. The only way I could
fly that aircraft was for Dean to climb out of his seat and let me take over.
But there was no way he planned to let a green pilot fly, as long as he himself was healthy. Without dual controls, there was no seat for the second
dickie. If I was to take full advantage of this trip, I must stand beside the
pilot and wireless operator all the way to and from the target. I was not
expected to perform any useful function, and the fact that they had a spare
pilot in case anything happened to their pilot was offset by their supersti-
tions that my coming along was ominous. Crews hated to take along a second dickie. You might say I was an observer who went along for the ride.

The second trip, with Flying Officer Armitage, like the first, was not
especially eventful. There is no way to simulate a bombing mission without being there. Night missions were flown in total darkness and complete
radio silence. The only voice heard was that of the pilot — and not too
often. The navigator would cut in with course changes, and occasionally
the wireless operator would speak up. Of course, the gunners would cut in
immediately in the event of a fighter attack.

Before we had crossed the English coast on this second trip, I heard the
navigator tell the pilot he was receiving ambiguous radar signals. What a
helluva way to start out. We were still over England and in navigational
trouble. The pilot cooled him down. Later he was able to pick up a new
signal from another location. For the bombing crew it was a lonely experience, and we tried to stay alert in the complete darkness. The red light on
the panel indicating that the undercarriage was in the "up" position was
usually too bright, so the pilot covered it with chewing gum.

The course had numerous changes so that the enemy was uncertain as
to what city was under attack. Altitude had to be changed frequently so

that ground installations would be confused as to the level of the bombing stream. The darkness was so intense I could see no one near, but I was constantly looking for any sign of danger. The voice of the navigator finally came on and said, "Skipper, in approximately five minutes the target will light up slightly off your port. I will give you the final countdown."

The bombardier left the navigation station and took his position in the nose over the bombsight, setting the height, speed, and direction on his equipment. He was ready to make any final corrections as we neared the target.

"Thirty seconds!" called out the navigator, and eventually, "Ten, nine, eight, seven, six, five, four, three, two, one – NOW!"

Immediately the sky lit up with the flares from the Pathfinders who were marking the target, and the master bomber came on the air to take control of the attack. I saw hundreds of aircraft all around us and realized they had been there all the time, although we were unable to see them. I thought to myself that it had to be a miracle that all the bombing stream had arrived at this designated time without colliding with another aircraft en route to the target.

At the moment when the pilot could no longer see the target area because it had disappeared under the nose of the aircraft, the bombardier would take over, directing him into the target: "Left, left, steady . . . a little right; hold it."

All around us flak was bursting. I wondered why the pilot was not attempting to dodge it. I found out later that in barrage flak an aircraft takes its chances, for it could dodge one burst and run into another.

At this point the bombardier had the target lined up in his bombsight. He listened for any final instructions from the master bomber. The bomb doors were open, and we were on the bombing run. No one interfered as the pilot froze on the exact course, speed, and altitude the bombardier had programmed into the bombsight. Here again one interruption was allowed — the gunners; self preservation came first. The bombardier pushed the bombing tit, and the wiper arm moved across the quadrant, releasing the bombs in sequence while the pilot maintained straight, level flight.

"Bombs gone," said the bombardier.

The engineer pulled the jettison toggle just in case any of the bombs had not released. We did not plan to take any of them home with us. The bomb doors closed, and the navigator gave the pilot a course for home. Flak continued to burst all around us before, during, and after the bombing run, and we were amazed that more of it did not hit our aircraft. On the way home we took the same care, trying to stay alert in the event of trouble.

What an experience! I was finally ready to do the same thing with my own crew. What a story I had to tell them. Flying Officer Armitage and his crew were happy they got home safely and that the second dickie pilot had not jinxed them.

Of the 107 aircraft on the raid, 1 aircraft from Six Group did not return.

One of World War II's unsung heroes, Murray Peden, in *A Thousand Shall Fall*, provides an analogy of what it was like to fly in a bomber at night and of the strain on the pilot and crew:

> To a person wanting to visualize how intense the strain could become, how suppressed fear could swell and gnaw inside, I offer the following as a comparison, perhaps easier to imagine than the unfamiliar surroundings of a darkened bomber cockpit framed in faintly luminous dials.
>
> Imagine yourself in a building of enormous size, pitch black inside. You are ordered to walk very slowly from one side to the other, then back. This walk in the dark will take you perhaps five or six hours. You know that in various nooks and crannies along your route killers armed with machine guns are lurking. They will quickly become aware that you have started your journey, and will be trying to find you the whole time you are in the course of it. There is another rather important psychological factor: the continuous roar emanating from nearby machinery. It precludes the possibility of your getting any audible warning of danger's approach. You are thus aware that if the trouble you are expecting does come, it will burst upon you with the startling surprise one can experience standing in the shower and having someone abruptly jerk open the door of the steamy cubicle and shout over the noise. If the killers stalking you on your walk should happen to detect you, they will leap at you out of the darkness firing flaming tracers from their machine guns. Compared with the armament they are carrying,

E-Easy — a close-up of "I'm Easy," coming home from our first trip.

you are virtually defenceless. Moreover, you must carry a pail
of gasoline and a shopping bag full of dynamite in one hand. If
someone rushes at you and begins firing, about all you can do
is fire a small calibre pistol in his direction and try to elude him
in the dark. But these killers can run twice as fast as you, and if
one stalks and catches you, the odds are that he will wound and
then incinerate you, or blow you into eternity. You are acutely
aware of these possibilities for every second of the five or six
hours you walk in the darkness, braced always, consciously or
subconsciously, for a murderous burst of fire, and reminded of
the stakes of the game periodically by the sight of guns flashing
in the dark and great volcanic eruptions of flaming gasoline.
You repeat this experience many times — if you live. (425)

I repeated it 13 of the 19 trips.

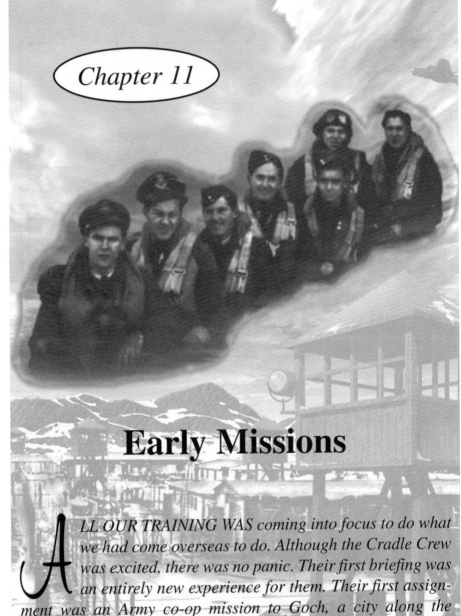

Chapter 11

Early Missions

*A**LL OUR TRAINING WAS** coming into focus to do what
we had come overseas to do. Although the Cradle Crew
was excited, there was no panic. Their first briefing was
an entirely new experience for them. Their first assign-*
ment was an Army co-op mission to Goch, a city along the
Rhine. Occasionally the military would ask for air support in
softening up the front lines. When this occurred, it was obvious
that the Army was meeting stiff ground resistance and had asked
for needed air support. Once the operation was called, the
ground forces had to hold their present position until the air

attack was completed. There were occasions, however, between the time air support was called for and the time the actual air operation took place, when the ground forces had been able to move forward. When this happened, the mission had to be aborted. This happened on at least one of our missions.

The Cradle Crew had an opportunity to witness firsthand the planning that went into an individual raid. The excitement continued after briefing and undoubtedly got us out to the dispersal considerably earlier than was necessary. The entire crew helped the ground crew bomb up the aircraft. Each crew member checked his equipment to make sure it was in perfect working order. This was no exercise. This was the real thing. When the guns were fired this time, they would have an enemy fighter in their sights. The bombs we were going to drop would do more than create a puff of smoke on the ground. The bombs and the armament were deadly, and the crew knew it. It was somber excitement.

We could not wait to get airborne. We were a typical green crew.

At 408 Squadron we had two 6,000-foot runways and one 4,500-foot runway. Interestingly, the bomb dump, where all the bombs were stored, was located just beyond the end of the short runway — nice planning.

During training at some of the stations, the ground crew would fill the bomb bay with sand bags to simulate the effect of a bomb load in the bomb bay. Unfortunately, our crew was never given such training. The Halifax started down the runway with the tail down, and as the speed developed, the tail came up. It was necessary for the tail to be in the "up" position to develop sufficient speed for takeoff. I hid my concern from the rest of the crew when we were told to take off on the short 4,500-foot runway. Our 8,000 pounds of bombs made a considerable difference in the takeoff, particularly when I had never experienced the effect of the additional weight before. With this added weight, more pressure was required on the steering column to make the tail rise. And in addition to having only a short runway to work with, I had the concern about the bomb dump just off the end of the runway — not a place I would like to make a crash landing. It was a hairy experience, but we made it. We would have no worry at all when we later used the long runways.

Our aircraft that night was *E for Easy*, and the date was February 7, 1945. For the Cradle Crew, this was it!

Because of our eagerness to get airborne, we had to orbit our station for

The enemy airfield Vokel was pock-marked after an attack by aircraft of the RCAF's Six Bomber Group in Britain during World War II.

a while before it was time to set course for our target. Knowing that the aircraft from 408, 426, and 425 Squadrons were also in this orbit made the ordeal more nerve-racking. All these aircraft were circling with no set plan, purely putting in time until they set course, and there was considerable danger of collision. On future missions we would find out how long it would take to get to course altitude and would determine our takeoff time accordingly.

Once in the air everyone was calm, but nervous, and each one hoped that I had learned enough on my two trips to take them to and from the target safely. The experience of the two second dickies paid off; I was able to keep the crew relatively relaxed for its first trip over enemy territory. Everything went well, and when we returned, some of the edge had been removed from their nervousness.

The following day Paris dateline read: "Kleve and Goch were bombed in great strength last night."

Of the 200 aircraft from Six Group, all returned safely.

My second trip to Wanne-Eickel occurred February 8, 1945, but this time I had my own crew with me. Our target was the synthetic oil plant, and the night mission brought the Cradle Crew into some predicted flak. Fortunately, the tail gunner, Ray Hughes, was alert, and he noticed the bursts getting closer. He quickly broke in on the intercom, and I did some slight evasive action, which avoided the possible danger.

There were 98 aircraft from Six Group, and 1 did not make it back.

On February 13 and 14 we made two more night missions, the first target a benzene plant at Bohlen in east-central Germany; the second, Chemnitz, in southeastern Germany. Both trips, on consecutive nights, were more than nine hours. For at least half the time, we were over enemy territory.

From Six Group, 115 aircraft attacked Bohlen, and all returned safely.

None of our targets were easy, but two of the more interesting runs were to Chemnitz, which was renamed Karl-Marx-Stadt after the war. Our first trip was on February 14, 1945; our target was to "wipe out the town." Chemnitz was a heavily industrialized area filled with military installations and personnel.

This night mission was our last trip before we got our own aircraft. It took nine hours and five minutes from takeoff to touchdown, with more than half of it over enemy territory. The target had been lit up by flares from Mosquitos and Lancasters of the Pathfinders, and we were on the bombing run when all of a sudden my bombardier yelled, "We are all screwed up, and we'll have to orbit and make another run at it!"

"What do you want me to do? Back up?"

I must have been out of my mind, for I decided to make another run. We were in the middle of some 650 aircraft, and I was making a 360-degree turn! During half the orbit it was like driving the wrong way on a busy one-way street. Our aircraft flew directly into the bombers who were behind us. The bombing stream behind us, noticing a plane going the opposite direction, could have mistaken us for a German fighter and shot at us. I had our aircraft in a 60-degree bank, hoping against hope I could make it back over the target area without colliding with another aircraft. Fortunately, our bombsight was capable of compensating for a severe banking action. Flak was bursting all around us, and while we did not meet any fighters, we knew they were there. Finally I could level out, and we made the second run over the target. The good Lord was watching over us, and we pulled through unscathed. I was never so happy to hear, "Bombs gone."

Six Group had 118 of the 650 total aircraft on this mission. It had to be sheer stupidity to do an orbit in the middle of the bombing stream. We got away with it, but that was the last time I ever tried that maneuver.

Three of our aircraft were not as fortunate.

E.Q.-Johnny.

The mission on February 18 was an Army co-op daylight raid on Wesel, the gateway to the industrial Ruhr Valley, in west-central Germany. Cloud over the target area was so dense that the mission was called off by the master bomber, who was concerned that the bombing would come too close to our advancing military. Unfortunately, we were carrying a long-delay "cookie" — a 4,000-pound bomb. Unlike the ordinary bombs we usually carried, which were instantaneously fused, they had to be dropped before they could be detonated. This one had been triggered before we took off, to detonate at a given hour. The principal was that the bomb would hit the target and then explode hours later. In any event, we had no intention of taking it back home.

There was a designated area in the North Sea for getting rid of any excess bomb load, and we headed for it. All ships at sea were aware of this area and made sure they kept well away. Since it was daylight, the crew wanted me to fly at a low altitude so that they could witness the explosion

when the bomb load hit the water. Atky told me he would release the
bombs on the normal wiper arm once the bomb doors were open, keeping
the aircraft steady. Unsuspecting, I was completely surprised when he
released the load with the toggle switch, and the kite jumped up and got
my attention real fast. I wondered what had happened; he and the rest of
the crew thought this was quite a gag to pull on me.

All 110 from Six Group that had participated returned.

One reason the Cradle Crew wanted the last trip to be a daylight was to
do a traditional "shoot up" of the station upon our return. The most memorable one to my recollection was when three of the squadron — Ed Finch,
LeRoy Pitou, and David Sokoloff — were on a daylight for their 30th mission. They orbited the station long enough for the rest of us to land and
watch their shoot up. Days before, they had scanned the station to determine just how they were going to do it. The Halifax is a heavy bomber that
does not have the maneuverability of a fighter plane, and after a severe
dive, there is a "mushing" action before the aircraft starts to climb again.
The pilot had better allow for this when considering a shoot up.

Ed Finch was first, and he made a noble effort. Dave Sokoloff dove at
the tower and pulled up as close as he dared. LeRoy Pitou tried to do him
one better. As I recall, they all did an outstanding job. The commanding
officer and David's wife, Emmy, were both in the tower at the time, and
Emmy said, "It's worse than giving birth." That was the end of shooting
up the home station.

Our second trip to Chemnitz (I'm afraid I can't get used to calling it
Karl-Marx-Stadt) was on March 5. This time before setting course we ran
into the edge of a squall while we were still orbiting over our station.
These squalls, occurring primarily in the winter months, came in unexpectedly off the North Sea. Should an aircraft be caught up in one, severe
icing could occur, causing the aircraft to become uncontrollable and possibly to crash. We were orbiting in dense clouds that surrounded the

E.Q.-Johnny with the ground crew.

squall, and I saw several of our kites go down, which was unnerving for those who escaped it. When I noticed an aircraft in trouble I would ask the navigator to "take the time please." He knew it meant to "take a fix on our position, I have just seen an aircraft go down."

On our return our base was fogged in, and we were diverted to Mildenhall in Suffolk, east of our airfield. It had been a long trip — 9 hours and 18 minutes, with 6 hours and 30 minutes entirely on instruments. Our fuel gauges read empty when we were given permission to land, but Doug Grey, our engineer, assured me he had calculated the petrol and we were still OK. We had not informed the rest of the crew members, who were in the belly of the aircraft. When Jim Taylor, our navigator, came forward to see why we were taking so long getting permission to land, he spotted the empty fuel gauges and let everyone know we were in deep doo doo. I tried to reassure him, but I was too busy with the landing procedure. As we made our last cross-wind leg, the starboard outer engine started to sputter. Immediately I feathered the prop, which takes it out of action. At the same time, I opened the throttles to see if I could get the aircraft to climb to 1,000 feet, because it looked like Doug had boobed and we were going to have to jump. Four-engine Halifax bombers do not glide to a landing if they run out of fuel; they drop out of the sky like broken elevators in the Empire State Building.

At 1,000 feet we were still OK on the three engines, so I was hesitant to give the order to jump. But instead of doing another complete circuit, I decided to take a shortcut over the tower when the port outer engine gave up the ghost. I feathered it and called the tower, "Bargeman Johnny — two engines."

They replied, "What is your problem?"

"I haven't time to tell you," I replied.

"Shoot off a Very cartridge when you are in the funnel."

The gun for the Very cartridge is located in the roof of the aircraft. Doug fired it, lighting up the night sky like a Roman candle. The tower then called all other aircraft to hold their positions until further notice. The funnel is the area where the plane last turns in to make its final approach. The flare allowed the ground forces to spot us; they would alert the fire command in the event of a crash. Usually when I was coming in for a landing the crew liked to kid me from their perch in the middle of the aircraft with comments like, "I'm standing on one foot; see if you can land without knocking me off balance."

This time there was no humor, only complete silence, as Doug and I brought our "two-engine aircraft" closer to the ground. The two inner engines were screaming. My lips were paper dry. I expected at any moment one of the two engines would conk out, because I had them at full throttle, and they were sucking up the petrol fast. If one more went, that would be all she wrote.

My landing was better than expected. When the ground crew refueled us the next day, one member told us we had "a couple of cups of petrol left." That was too close for comfort.

Of the 183 aircraft from Six Group, 6 did not return.

One of my responsibilities after we had landed at a strange station was to make sure my crew was billeted properly. Mildenhall had more than it could handle that night, and after my Cradle Crew was all settled, the only place left for me to sleep was on the pool table. It was hard as hell. If you doubt it, try it.

The next morning the crew thought we should leave Mildenhall with some small memento of our visit; they talked me into "shooting up" the station. This was not exactly a recommended procedure, but as a safety precaution we decided to shoot it up across the runway in use. When we started the shoot up at about 1,500 feet, a small fighter plane was landing. In turning off, he placed himself directly in my line for the shoot up. Guess he figured I was some kind of a nut, attempting to land on a runway that was used for taxiing. As we got close to the ground, he pulled off onto the grass. He was sure we were one brick shy of a load. It was a momentary thrill; once it was over we headed back to our base.

At that time of year English weather conditions were unpredictable, and on our return from a mission it was not uncommon to be diverted to a different station because the weather at Linton-on-Ouse had closed in.

It bothered me to be wearing my flying helmet when we entered another station, so I started taking along my officer's hat. After entering through the hatch at the rear of the Halifax, I would place my officer's hat on a tank containing nitrogen gas that was fed into the petrol tanks to reduce the possibility of explosion. The top of this tank was about the size of my head. Then I would don my flying helmet.

Occasionally our home base at Linton received diverted American aircraft when their own station was fogged in. The American aircrew all wore fleeced-lined jackets, which all Canadian and British aircrew envied. On the other hand, Canadian and British aircrew all wore knee-high, fleece-lined flying boots, which the American crews envied over their short, unlined flying boots. It was not uncommon to see one or two of the American airmen wandering back to their aircraft in their shirtsleeves, wearing knee-high flying boots the following morning. Padre McLeod had a fleece-lined jacket, but he refused to tell us how he had acquired it. He would try to distract us with another subject like, "Amazing people these British. They invent a Spitfire on one hand and can only develop a pull-chain toilet on the other."

The pilot of a Halifax sat immediately above the wireless operator; he had to climb up to get into his seat. It was wise to perform toilet necessities before setting forth, but on some of the longer trips there was a limit to how long the pilot could manage before he had to relieve himself. Neither the pilot nor the crew was happy when the pilot elected to go to the portable john in the rear.

To eliminate the necessity of getting out of the seat and going to the back of the aircraft, there was a small hose for his personal use. But many pilots, finding this too difficult to manage, took the pan-like cover off the back of the auto-pilot and used it instead. One of the crew was elected to dump it. Unfortunately, an air pocket often would rock the aircraft at this inopportune moment, and the wireless operator would be christened as he operated his radio below. This never happened in our aircraft, however. Three of our missions were nine hours or longer, and I was turning yellow by the time we had landed.

The gunners on bombers, particularly at night, had a tension-packed assignment, sitting alone in a turret with instructions not to talk unless there was trouble developing. It was difficult, first of all, to keep wide awake looking out into complete blackness. From time to time he might think he saw something unusual, but he would hesitate, to make sure. Other Allied aircraft in the raid could be all around; in the darkness they would appear only as dark objects — were they friendly aircraft or German night fighters? One mistake and the entire crew could be lost.

Inside the aircraft the wireless operator scanned his Fishpond, a small screen on which other aircraft appeared as a blip. When the aircraft was in the middle of the bombing stream, this was not too meaningful.

Night operations were done in total darkness from start to finish. When we returned we were directed to a specific dispersal area. Shortly, a lorry would arrive, often half loaded with crew members picked up at other dispersals. We would all climb aboard with our gear, and the driver usually remarked, "Anyone not aboard please say so." With this, he would drive off.

A routine item we were furnished on every mission was an escape kit. It consisted of maps, compasses, Horlick tablets for energy, and other items we might require should we be forced down in enemy territory. We were always somewhat blasé about the kits; we hoped we would never have to put them to use. During the mission we carried the packet inside our battle dress; it was something we wanted immediately available in an emergency.

Our crew makeup during operations was three officers and four sergeants. The officers lived on the station, and the NCOs lived in Benningborough Hall, some distance away. The NCOs had to rely on a lorry to transport them to and from the squadron. Atky, Jim, and I, the three officers, had a room on the station; Doug, Wat, Curly, and Brock lived in the hall. There were some extra bunks in our room, so whenever we had a dance, the NCOs would stay in our room. They kept some of their clothing with us in case they had to clean up for some activity. One night when there was a dance, Curly had just come out of the shower. Before starting to dress he asked for my black shoe polish. I imagined he was going to shine his dress shoes. Wrong. He took the brush and blackened his heels. (One was never sure what Curly was up to; this was definitely one of those times.) A few moments later he put on his black socks; both had a large hole in the back. "That works out great!" he said. "You have to look real close to see the hole."

Chapter 12

Time Off — Then Back to Work

W
E ALWAYS LOOKED FORWARD to a leave. At the
outset, Atky and I would go off on our own, but later
on the entire Cradle Crew would select a spot, and
we would stay together.

There was an English family with whom Atky and I became
well acquainted, and we spent several leaves with them. Ralph
Petley was a retired race car driver who had lost one eye, and
his wife Dorothy was a great storyteller. This was a second mar-
riage for both of them. It was obvious that Ralph enjoyed
Dorothy's commanding most of the conversation. He was a great

listener. They lived in Henley-in-Arden, not far from Stratford-on-Avon.

Henley-in-Arden was a small village; its two major attractions were pubs — one at each end of the village. The Bird-in-Hand and the Blue Bell had been in operation for many years before we got there; they are still operating today, no doubt under new owners. (When I say in operation "for many years," it would be more accurate to say "for several hundred years.") To acknowledge their many kindnesses, Atky and I sometimes treated the Petleys to dinner out, usually at one of these pubs.

The Petleys had a beautiful home. Every morning before we awoke, Dorothy polished our shoes and shined our buttons — first class. Ralph drove a Bentley and loved to take us out on the Great North Road and open it up. They often used their ration coupons to buy items for us, and always had plenty of cold milk — so much better than the milk on the station.

We had to provide Air Command with the name or names of persons to be notified if something happened to us. The Petleys asked that we include their names along with those of our parents, fiancees, and relatives. After we returned to England from our stay at Stalag Luft 1, Dorothy told us that when she had been informed that we were "missing," she had bought two potted plants and named one of them Atky and the other Ken. She took good care of them, and to console herself she had decided as long as the plants were alive we would be alive as well. Unfortunately, one of the plants died — the one named for Atky. She presumed that he had been killed, which, fortunately, was not so. (Ironically, however, Atky was the first Cradle Crew member to die. Would you believe, he had a heart attack at the 1963 Grey Cup championship football game in Vancouver, British Columbia. Another piece of irony: Curly was at that same game; he saw a person being carried out and assumed it was someone who had had "one too many." He found out later it was Atky.)

One of our leaves took us to London. Nobody goes to England without visiting London, a city brimming with history. Londoners feel they should apologize for anything that is not at least 200 years old. The crew and I were walking in the area of the House of Commons when we saw a clock

The Petleys with Atky — Dorothy, Ralph, and Nancy.

that I assumed was connected with the Houses of Parliament. I saw a British WAC coming along the street, and I asked her, "Is that clock over there correct?"

"Correct?" she asked indignantly, fire coming out of her eyes. "Of course it's correct – it's Big Ben!"

Oops, my mistake. Somehow I had thought Big Ben would be larger, somewhat along the lines of the clock on the Parliament Buildings in Ottawa. Dumb Canadian. Well, you can't know everything.

After our much-needed leaves, we returned to our station.

Some of the earlier Halifax aircraft had Merlin engines. The Mark II was so equipped. Though the Merlins were superb on the Lancasters, they just did not have the power required for the Halifaxes. On takeoff the Halifax seemed to need an eternity to get to the required altitude. In general, it did not have the maneuverability of the later Mark Halifaxes.

One of my closest friends overseas was Earl "Pop" Tait. We had both received our wings at #4 Service Flying Training School. We went overseas together, but eventually they split us up. Pop Tait had developed his nickname, not because he had a large family like Doug Grey, but because he had an extremely dark beard, which gave him the appearance of being much older than his years. On a training mission at Wombleton, Pop and his crew attempted unsuccessfully to climb over a thundercloud. They crashed. Inside these cumulonimbus clouds there were vicious icing conditions coupled with extreme updrafts and downdrafts, which could virtually tear an aircraft apart. I always felt that his flying a Mark II Halifax contributed to this incident. The later Mark Halifaxes had the ability to climb to a higher ceiling, which might have permitted him to fly over the thundercloud, as we had to do on one occasion.

It was our good fortune to fly the latest Handley Page Halifax, a Mark VII. To my knowledge they never built a later model. The Mark VII was powered by four Bristol Hercules 16 engines, each delivering more than 1,650 horsepower. This Halifax had an improved all-around performance, with a quicker takeoff, an increased rate of climb, a greater top speed and cruising speed at operational altitude, and a higher ceiling. On takeoff, our all-up weight was 65,000 pounds.

The armament consisted of one Vickers Gas Operated gun in the nose and four .303 machine guns in both the mid-upper and rear turrets. Squadron activity included practice, when no raids were scheduled. On one such exercise, we dropped a smoke bomb in the North Sea. The tail and mid-upper gunners attempted to sink it as we made our runs back and forth over the area. At that moment the enemy was safe — the smoke bomb continued to belch forth its smoke. Neither of our experienced gunners could hit the target. Atky took a turn with the VGO in the nose turret, and he, too, had no luck. Wat then asked for a turn with the VGO. I told him I would fly our kite as low as possible to see if he could make a "kill." I made the run, and Wat hit the smoke bomb and sank it. He was so excited he told the gunners and Atky, "I'll be giving lessons once we land, and I would suggest all three of you take advantage of my talents."

Atky and Ken Blyth in the Bentley.

Later Curly told me I was so low for Wat's run that he was getting splashed with salt water in the rear turret.

Earlier versions of the Halifax had already been operational in the Battle of Berlin; however, no Berlin raids were made during my stay on the squadron. From Six Group Berlin would be about the maximum range, which usually resulted in sacrificing bomb load for fuel.

In comparing the Halifax to the Lancaster there were two schools of thought. The Lancaster was sleeker, and it had better fuel consumption and, therefore, longer range. It was possibly more maneuverable in flight. However, one major disadvantage it had, to my mind, was the large main spar running through the middle of the aircraft, which the crew had to climb over if they had to abandon the plane. Should the aircraft be in a dive or some evasive action, the centrifugal force could make it difficult for the crew to get over this main spar to get to the escape hatch.

The Halifax, on the other hand, had no such problems. It was a sturdy piece of equipment; it could take a considerable pounding, yet remain air-worthy. In most books on the war, the Lancaster was given top billing, but I never found any Halifax pilots who complained that the Halifax was not first string. I would add that if for some reason it was necessary to land immediately after takeoff, it could not be done until the plane had used up a considerable amount of petrol or the crew had jettisoned the bombs because the undercarriage could not handle an all-up weight of 65,000 pounds.

One feature of both the Lancaster and Halifax aircraft was the huge tires. They were about 4½ to 5 feet high. Today's aircraft tires are small by comparison. Part of our external check before takeoff included close examination of these tires. They had inner tubes with the nipple protruding. On the tire rim a small rectangle was painted around the nipple, which would center your check on whether or not the inner tube had shifted and was pulling on the nipple. On every landing, as the tires hit the runway, there could be a small shift between the inner tube and the outer tire. This shift was particularly important if the pull became too great. At this point the action of landing could snap off the nipple, and a blow-out would occur. That would be all she wrote. This happened to a close friend of mine from Ottawa who had completed three quarters of a tour; the entire crew was wiped out. Needless to say, Doug and I closely inspected our tires, and if the nipple had shifted, we made the aircraft unserviceable.

On the bombing run only the bombardier could see the target when we were approximately five minutes from the target. He lay on his stomach in the nose of the aircraft with his eyes peering into the bombsight, holding the bomb tit in his right hand. The bomb doors were open, and only the bombardier controlled the bomb release. The bomb tit was connected to the wiper arm, which had 16 "stations," each controlling one 500-pound bomb. The wiper arm controlled the release of the bombs. When the bombardier squeezed the bomb tit, the wiper arm operated similarly to the windshield wiper on a car. As it contacted each of the 16 stations, a bomb was released. The pattern was one from the front of the bomb bay, one from the back, the sequence continuing this pattern until all the bombs were released. This particular pattern permitted the aircraft to remain stable throughout the bombing run. The pilot's function on the run was to concentrate on maintaining a set speed, direction, and height. All these factors were programmed into the bombsight. Any minor deviation would interfere with the accuracy of the bombing run.

Peanut-butter-and-jelly sandwiches were a popular packed lunch we took along on missions. The station mess always provided several peppermint-filled chocolate bars as well. I never did like peanut butter, so I would usually end up with just a jelly sandwich and several chocolate bars. We were always given several "Waky Waky" pills in the event we became drowsy, but I do not recall that we ever used many of them. Wat had a bottle he kept his pills in, and being a Scotsman with a "waste not, want not" philosophy, he collected them from the crew and had them available for other events, should the need arise. On one occasion when we had returned from a mission just before a dance, Wat provided us with at least two pills each to make sure we had a good time at the dance. Then the dance was canceled! Wat, Curly, Brock, and Doug stayed in our room on the station and kept us awake by talking all night. So much for Waky Waky pills, today's No-Doz.

Our ninth mission was to Hemmingstedt, or Dessau, in east-central Germany, southwest of Berlin, and our target was an oil refinery. En route we experienced icing over the English Channel. The pitot head, located just below the nose cone, iced up, causing my air speed indicator to show that our speed was falling off. Because this came without warning, it momentarily gave me the sensation the aircraft was going to stall. But when I pushed the nose down, the action dislodged the icing, and the air speed indicator corrected itself. We settled down and proceeded to the target without further incident. The target itself was lit up with many ground markers. It was an easy "do."

A clipping from an old London paper carries the item:

> More than 1250 RAF and RCAF planes — the largest night force flung from Britain this year — last night blasted the Germans' eastern front base of Dessau, struck at vital oil refineries. Five Canadian heavy bombers are missing.

Three of these missing bombers were from Six Group.

Regardless of the hour, the padres on the station were always on hand when we took off and returned. I can still see the Reverend Mac McLeod at the chalkboard marking down the aircraft numbers as they called in on their return to the circuit. He usually had all the planes listed and then checked in each one individually. Once we landed, one of the first things we would do was to check Mac's chalkboard to see who had not returned. I am sure the padres sent up a lot of prayers for us individually and collectively, particularly for those who did not return at that time. They would try to assure those of us who had returned that those who had not, had undoubtedly landed at another station. Most of the time they were not convincing. If a crew did not return with the stream, we felt it had "gone for a Burton," or had at least been captured.

Tradition had it that after checking in, we were "issued" a shot of rum. Four of the crew were non-drinkers, so the extra amounts were divided among the other three. It usually gave them a bit of a buzz. After debriefing we headed for the mess, where another tradition said that the King of England did not eat bacon and eggs until all active aircrew had been served theirs. I don't suppose anyone ever checked this out.

We made a successful raid on Hamburg, on the north German coast, the night of March 8, 1945. We approached the target area flying at about 2,000 feet over the North Sea, then climbed to our bombing altitude of 18,300 feet for the bombing run. Flak over the target was quieter than expected, and we could see lots of fires and explosions. Fortunately there were few fighters. Our trip was uneventful, except that on the return we were again flying low over the North Sea when I remembered it was Wat's 21st birthday. I had said nothing to the rest of the crew and did not know whether they were aware of it. As radio operator, Wat could not hear the crew's conversations without cutting himself back in. When I flashed him on the intercom light, he asked, "What's up, skipper?"

Immediately, the entire Cradle Crew started singing "Happy Birthday." It was an emotional moment, but he appreciated it. He told me afterwards that he had just written in his wireless log "0001, I am now 21." Our practical-joker crew could not leave it at that, however. When we got back to the squadron and reported to briefing, I raced to the Wireless Section before Wat and approached his flight leader. I told him to tell Wat "Happy Birthday," and when Wat asked how he knew, to explain he had left his radio "open," and the entire tower had heard us serenading him. Such an error was a mortal sin for a wireless operator. We let Wat suffer with this for a while before we told him it was a gag.

One crew from Six Group did not return.

We made two interesting raids on March 11 and 12. The first was to Essen, in the heart of the heavily defended Ruhr Valley. The operation utilized 1,000 aircraft, 196 of these from Six Group. Overall, it was a beautiful day with a minimum of flak. We were flying in a gaggle, a technique employed by the British and Canadian forces on most of their daylight missions. There were three lead aircraft flying in a vee, similar to the flight of Canadian geese. The balance of the stream positioned themselves behind, in accordance with their target designated time. We jockeyed for position well in the center of the gaggle for safety reasons. Each navigator, of course, had to continue his own activity, to make sure we reached the target at our appointed time. We usually had fighter protection for part of the way to the target, but seldom all the way. Enemy fighters rarely entered the gaggle, preferring to stay outside and attempt to knock off those aircraft on the edge of the stream. Because the formation was very tight, one of the problems encountered was that we would hit air pockets caused by the other aircraft. Although it was not formation flying as such, it was close enough to it.

On this particular day, as we neared the target, my engineer drew my attention to the fact that there was an aircraft immediately above me, and we were not far apart. I quickly moved to my port. You guessed it — so did the pilot above. It was a checker game: whatever direction I decided to take, the pilot above would do the same thing. It was humorous for a while, and that "while" was until he opened the bomb doors. We were now looking up at 16 500-pound bombs. It didn't take long for me to decide to move several widths this time. When the bombs were finally dropped, Doug Grey was watching closely. We were far enough away for them not to give us too much concern. Actually, bombs fall behind the aircraft and never straight down. That is great information, but very little assurance when you are directly beneath them. It's not a time to test the theory.

Two from Six Group did not return.

The following day we attacked Dortmund, southwest of Hamburg, not far from Cologne, with 1,100 aircraft, 192 from Six Group. Once again the flak was light. With this many aircraft on the mission, the target was "open" for 33 minutes. It is hard to imagine. From above one looks down and sees the bombs against the clouds; they look like pepper on a white blanket.

All Six Group aircraft returned safely.

Falling into air pockets was always a frightening experience. In the air pocket the pilot had little or no control of the aircraft. Most often the fall occurred when we met up with the slipstream of another aircraft. It was possible to drop some 100 to 150 feet in a matter of seconds. In the middle of the gaggle on a daylight raid, air pockets were commonplace, for we were more inclined to fly a tighter formation. At night they would scare the hell out of us, because we knew other aircraft were close by, and we wondered how we had missed hitting one of them.

After the Cradle Crew had completed ten missions we were invited to join the Pathfinders Squadron. We declined for two reasons: First, it meant another three months of intensive training, and we did not envy that. Second, it was felt, generally, that the war was drawing to a close, and we were anxious to complete our tour. At any other time we would have accepted.

The Pathfinders did a yeomanlike job, and theirs was a dangerous assignment. They went ahead of the bombing stream to mark the target. Their activity over the target took place usually at low altitude, making it doubly dangerous. Sometimes the marking was done with ground flares, and when we had heavy cloud cover they used sky markers. The colors were varied: one time we might bomb on "double red with green"; another time it could be "double green with double yellow." The enemy tried to confuse us by lighting up bogus targets and dropping sky markers of their own. Often it was necessary for the master bomber to change the colors and change the headings for bombing due to wind changes. Without the Pathfinders it is questionable how successful our night missions and many of our daylight missions would have been.

In order to provide the bombing stream with as much protection as possible, Group Command commissioned 100 Group to create a diversionary force to detract the enemy as long as possible. Their mission was to assist the bombing stream in getting to and from the target safely. The Stirling bomber was used extensively in this type of operation. One of the techniques was to set up a Mandrel screen, which emitted signals that caused a snow effect on the German Freyas radar equipment. Another technique used by 100 Group was to operate within the bombing stream, and when the stream made a course change, several of 100 Group would continue straight ahead dropping "window" (strips of foil) in volumes that prevented the German radar from distinguishing which was the bomber stream and which was the decoy. This would be done at each course change, and sometimes when no change was indicated. Without such protection by 100 Group, our losses would have been substantially greater.

By March 14 we had made six trips over enemy territory in nine days. This time it was Zweibrücken, in the Ruhr Valley, an unusual situation, because the target was totally clear and we were able to bomb visually. Fighters and flak were almost nonexistent.

An undocumented article from a British newspaper described it:

British bombers thundered into action last night. Heavies attacked Zweibrücken and Homberg, about 15 miles east of

Saarbrücken, in an effort to wipe out troops and military stores reported concentrated in these two towns.

All 196 aircraft from Six Group returned home safely.

On March 16 we were engaged in a night operation to Hagen, in west-central Germany, not far from the Netherlands border. While the target was well lighted and the flak moderate, we did get caught in the ground searchlights, warning us of impending night fighters or predicted flak. The German ground forces had the ability to calculate an aircraft's height, airspeed, and direction. With this information they produced and directed a cone of lights on a particular aircraft. One could have read an evening newspaper in the light of the cone at 20,000 feet. However, we did not have time to do that — the first order of business was to get out of the cone.

A rather simple maneuver of a slight weave and a lowering and climbing action usually allowed an aircraft to evade the lights. If it did not, slight adjustments on the German ground instruments would result in a direct hit by predicted flak or an attack by a night fighter. Ordinarily the ground flak was fired up in concentration with the hope that some of it would hit the attacking aircraft. That was called barrage flak, and generally we paid little or no attention to it. Trying to avoid it was pointless. The predicted flak was much more accurate and deadly. In practice, the predicted flak usually burst behind you and with each burst the flak got closer. If there were night fighters in the vicinity, they would be on the lookout for aircraft caught in the cone. And the lights were distracting to one's own gunners, making it difficult to spot the enemy fighter. For the night fighter, the bomber caught in the cone was like a duck in a shooting gallery.

Of the 142 aircraft from Six Group, 3 did not make it back.

A piece of defensive mechanism carried on every bomber was called "IFF": Identification — Friend or Foe. Allied ground forces in England were able to pick up aircraft that did not so identify themselves, such aircraft becoming fair game for the ground forces. Eventually over time, with Allied aircraft being shot down over enemy territory, the IFF equipment got into the hands of the enemy. Night fighters, so equipped, would "home" in on the bombing stream on its return from a mission and use the IFF equipment to cross the English coast, unnoticed, with the bombing stream. It was normal for most crews to become less vigilant after crossing the coast, for they felt they were clear of enemy attack. Suddenly, as they put on their lights in the circuit, they would be fair game for the Luftwaffe. To offset this possibility, Bomber Command varied our instructions as to whether the IFF should be on or off. The Jerries would have to assume we had it on.

Emphasis was placed on not only completing the mission but on doing so as close to the predetermined time as possible. Usually Bomber Command built in some extra time for a mission in case the winds became more severe than predicted and/or the aircraft met some hostile action en route. The navigator watched the time factor very closely, and when it looked like we had too much time to spare, he would propose a "dog leg." This was something like playing Chinese Checkers, for in order to arrive at a given point one went twice as far as necessary. Assuming a three-minute dog leg, the navigator would instruct the pilot to turn 60 degrees to starboard for three minutes, then 120 degrees port for three minutes, then back onto the original course. So it took six minutes to get to a point where without the dog leg it would have taken three. Damn clever, those navigators. However, there was one major problem on a night mission. Because there was no set time when you might decide to make a dog leg, in the extreme darkness there was a strong possibility you could fly into the path of another aircraft. We had several close calls, and I am sure aircraft went down as a result of a collision from one of them doing this maneuver.

Night missions were generally designed to hit the target area as close to dawn as possible. Air Command believed that the enemy was the least prepared for engagement at this hour. The three squadrons would set course from the Linton area while it was still daylight. We were a small attacking force, but as we proceeded south to the English Channel we would be joined from time to time by other squadrons. This was always impressive. Somehow the additional aircraft joining the stream made us feel we had an air armada crossing the enemy coast. Soon it was dark, and in the pitch black of the night we could see no one; as far as we were concerned, we were alone again. We flew several hours in this total darkness all the way to the target. Once the Pathfinders lit up the target, we could see aircraft all around us. It was awesome — and hard to believe the other planes had been so close all the time.

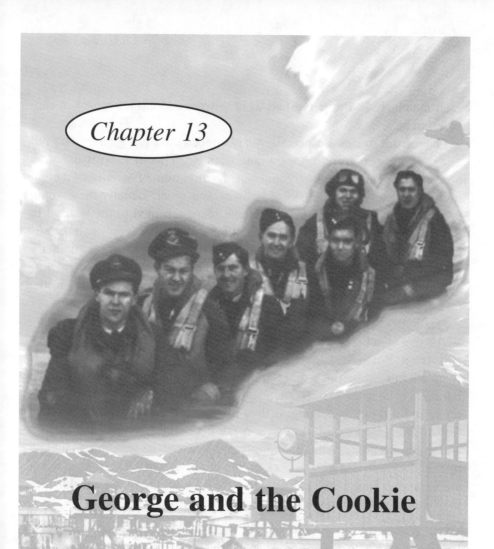

Chapter 13

George and the Cookie

*T*HE BRITISH AIR FORCES *had a monthly paper called* **Tee-Emm** *("Training Manual"). In it were recounted (after authentication) some of the weird events that had happened to Air Force personnel during World War II. I don't know how the Cradle Crew escaped being part of one of the stories. The favorite character in all of them was called Pilot Officer Percy Prune. His creator was Bill Hooper, who loved to doodle. Hooper's drawings, which had amused the pilots of 54 Fighter Squadron, Hornchurch, eventually developed into the* **Tee-Emm** *presentations that all aircrew waited impatiently for*

each month. P. O. Prune typified what officers and airmen were not supposed to be.

One of the stories I especially liked concerned a tail gunner who fell
asleep in the rear turret on a training exercise. This in itself was not an
unlikely happening, because gunners had a minimum of activity on a night
training exercise, and the sky was black and quiet. Usually they would
take 40 winks but "come to" before the plane returned to the station. In
this documented story our hero, P. O. Prune, was still asleep when the aircraft landed and taxied to a dispersal. I am sure the night was particularly
dark when the rest of the crew piled out of the Halifax at the dispersal area
and into a waiting lorry along with the crews from other aircraft. In the
darkness one sort of assumed everyone was there as the lorry headed for
the station.

All was quiet when the tail gunner finally awoke and thought he was
still flying. When he called the skipper on the intercom there was naturally no answer, so he flashed him on the signal light. When he got nothing
but silence, he came to the conclusion the crew had bailed out. He spun his
turret and fell out, expecting to float in space. The turret at rest is a few
feet off the ground, and in that short fall he managed to pull the ripcord
and sprain his ankle. Although totally embarrassed, he was able to bundle
up the parachute and hobble back to one of the hangars. There were many
embarrassing situations, and we can look back on them and chuckle, but
they were not very funny to the individual at the time.

Atky continued to look for an opportunity to fly the aircraft. On one
occasion we were over the English coast, well on our way home in the
early evening from a raid on Rheine when I was flying with the automatic pilot engaged. This had been one of our quieter trips, and on the
return the bombardier had little to do. The lever to engage or disengage the
automatic pilot was a short distance away from me on the steering column.
For safety's sake I rigged a strong cord to it and kept the other end in my
hand. In case of attack I could quickly pull the cord and disengage the
auto-pilot.

Atky was anxious to fly with "George," the auto-pilot, engaged. We
were discussing this without the benefit of the intercom, so the rest of

the crew were unaware of what we were up to. While I climbed down from my position and Atky climbed in, I explained that all he had to do was turn the little crank beside him forward if the nose of the aircraft started to go up, and turn it up if the nose started to go down. Simple enough; he could handle it. Actually, if one left the aircraft alone, when either of these events occurred it would right itself. But Atky had to use the crank, and thus I continued to keep the cord in my hands for a very good reason.

The aircraft without "George" engaged flew with the starboard wing low. When I engaged the auto-pilot, the aircraft flew with the port wing low. To make it fly straight and level with the auto-pilot, I had to accentuate the starboard low position when I engaged the automatic pilot. But I didn't give all that good info to Atky. He had enough to worry about trying to figure out how to turn the crank.

Before I knew it he was cranking down the lever, and we were in a severe dive. I shouted to him to crank it back. He did so, but he waited for the nose to start coming up. Next thing we knew we were in a steep climb. I shouted again to him to trap it and not wait for the action to happen. He got more confused by the minute, and we were going up and down like a teeter-totter. One moment Curly was looking at the sky above him, and the next moment he was staring at the ground. Atky was playing crack the whip with the tail gunner's neck. If I had pulled on the auto-pilot cord, it would have added a spiral action to all of Atky's other problems. Instead, I climbed up and over him to reach the automatic controls and stabilize the aircraft.

That was the last time he asked to fly. He learned later about the spiral action possibility, and he was thankful I had handled it the way I had. Once again the crew "suggested" that Atky not spend any more time than necessary in the pilot's seat.

Over the course of our numerous trips I would let each member of the crew who wanted to fly take over the controls for a few minutes at a time when the possibility of danger was limited. While they seemed to enjoy it, I noticed none of them asked for a second turn. It was about this time that I told the crew that if anything ever happened to me they should not let Atky talk them into trying to land our aircraft. Their interests would be better served if he could hold the aircraft straight and level while they all bailed out, then he followed them!

Rheine was the first of four continuous daylight raids. The second was to Dorsten, another gaggle formation, one of our easier missions. An undocumented newspaper account described it:

> Canadian heavies joined British four-engined aircraft in assaulting the communications centre of Rheine, near the 21st Army group front along the lower Rhine yesterday.

Rheine and Dorsten, near the west-central German border, were back-to-back raids on March 21 and 22. We had the following day off, and on the 24th attacked Gladbeck. Though it was another quiet "do," I did see the aircraft on my starboard quarter go down in flames. I couldn't tell whether or not it was from our squadron. I found out later it was not.

This was a good show. All 100 aircraft from Six Group returned safely.

From time to time we would be called on to carry a "cookie," a bomb that looked like a giant water heater. It was even shaped like a water heater, and it had a very slow terminal velocity. In other words, it fell to earth slowly. The regular bombs were streamlined, falling quickly. The danger in having a mixed load of bombs, including a cookie, was that the faster-falling 500-pound bombs would catch up with the cookie and detonate prematurely. To compensate for this, a peg was placed in the wiper arm panel. After the cookie went, the wiper arm stopped at the peg. Then the bombardier counted to ten before pulling the peg and allowing the balance of the bomb load to release. (The regular bombs have a propeller-like unit in the tail fin, which unscrews when released, releasing the detonator in the nose, allowing it to explode immediately upon impact. The cookie has a long delay action that permits it to explode sometime after it hits the target. The latter effect was particularly effective in penetrating large buildings.)

On March 25, a mission was called. To round up the Cradle Crew members, I drove the Flea to the Sergeants Mess, where I knew I would at least find Doug Grey playing craps and, hopefully, Wat, Ray, and Brock. A lorry was parked out front, and I thought to myself, "Don't park too close to that guy for he will not be able to see our small car, and he might back into it." I allowed myself what I felt was a reasonable distance and went inside to round up the crew. When I came out, lo and behold, if the clown hadn't backed into the Flea. The back of the lorry had crushed the radiator. When the driver found out he had done this to an officer's automobile, he felt sure he would be court-martialed. I let him know how high I thought his intelligence level ran, then left the Flea to be repaired at a later date. It never happened. After we returned from the prison camp, Atky went back to Linton and reported that someone had stolen the tires — the only worthwhile item on the Flea — but he was able to sell it for £12.

The target for this daylight raid was the Munster railroad yards — an excellent choice. We had a great view. In our bomb bay we carried a cookie. Barrage flak was moderate to intense. Upon our return, we were diverted to Leeming, Yorkshire, because of the weather conditions at our base.

Although the pilot is captain of the aircraft at all times en route and returning, the navigator dictates the routing and altitude to be followed. Should we be attacked at any time, the gunners can override any discussion that might be transpiring between any of the crew members. Usually the last five minutes or so of the bombing run the bombardier is in charge, directing the pilot visually, particularly once the target is out of the sight of the pilot and clearly in the view of the bombardier.

We were making our run on the Munster rail yards, and Atky was giving me the "left, left, steady" or "right, right, steady" when a burst of barrage flak exploded directly in front of us, and we immediately flew through a thick pall of black smoke. The nose of the aircraft seemed to be encased in it. Fortunately none of the shrapnel burst in our direction or it would have blown a gaping hole in the nose. A few minutes later, after we had dropped our bombs, Atky came out of the nose, heading for the back of the aircraft. When I asked him where he was going, he responded, "I'm going to check my drawers."

Just another close one.

On a more somber note, it was on this mission that one of our buddies from 408 was also carrying a cookie. But the bombardier either forgot to implant the peg or forgot to count to ten before releasing the peg. The unthinkable happened — the faster 500-pounders caught up with the cookie and detonated, blowing up the aircraft in action.

Besides our buddy and his crew, 2 other aircraft of the 99 from Six Group did not return from the raid.

When we had lived in Ottawa before the war, we had a newspaper delivery boy called Tucker Jenkins. Tucker, slightly older than I, lived down the street. He enlisted about the same time I did, but our paths never crossed until 408 Squadron. Would you believe he was in charge of the ground crew that loaded the bombs on our aircraft. We made a practice of helping the ground crew with this assignment, so they felt they were a part of the mission. From newspaper delivery boy to bomb delivery boy. Such somewhat trivial events or circumstances never ceased to amaze me.

We had to believe we were now professionals, and like professionals, although we were in battle operations, we still had to practice. March 27, 1945, found us doing a bombing exercise, together with Standard Beam Approach. The latter we never had to use.

Besides using flak and fighter aircraft, the Germans endeavored to demoralize the Allied fighter command with a radio program directed to a particular phase of the war. The voice was "Lord Haw Haw," who would threaten us with commentary such as, "We are ready to take care of you whiskey-drinking Canadian lumberjacks."

On March 31 they did just that.

Chapter 14

The Last Mission —
Beware of the Hun in the Sun

O N MARCH 31, 1945, Easter Saturday, Bomber Command had called a daylight raid with 460 heavy bombers on the Blohm & Voss prefabricated submarine pens at Hamburg. It looked like "a piece of cake" for my 19th mission. For the rest of the Cradle Crew, it was the 17th. The strategy was similar to our March 8 raid on the same target. It was one of the usual gaggle formations used for daylight raids, and this time there would be fighter cover.

We were to make a low-level sweep over the North Sea below 2,000 feet; then when we crossed the coast, we were to climb quickly to our designated bombing altitude. Several attempts had been made by both Canadian and American aircrews to eliminate these submarine pens, without success. Obviously our March 8 raid had not done the job. Sometime since that date American Fortresses had made a daylight attack on the same target. Our earlier raid had been a night sortie. Apparently both the raids had produced minimum damage, and we were going back to finish the job.

After our normal briefing we took our time getting airborne. There was no sense in rushing and then having to orbit over our station longer than necessary. Our orbit interlocked with both the 428 Thunderbird Squadron and the 425 Alouette Squadron. All three squadrons were part of Six Group, an all-Canadian group principally outfitted with Lancasters and Halifaxes.

Considerable time was allocated for the entire squadron to take off and orbit until the time designated to set course for the target. The newer crews, naturally excited, were always the first off, so they had to orbit for a prolonged period. But by this time, because of our experience we knew exactly how long it would take to get up to orbit altitude. We deliberately delayed our engine startup so that once we had climbed to flight altitude it would be time to set course, minimizing the considerable danger involved when three squadrons interlocked in the same orbit and circled aimlessly.

E.Q.-Johnny, our aircraft, had just come off inspection and should have been in great shape for this daylight raid. Flight Engineer Doug Grey and I had assisted the ground crew in bombing up. After completing our external inspection we climbed aboard to give the engines a run-up and to check the interior gauges before leaving the dispersal. Doug fussed over the instruments, because they were his specialty. Other than the flying instruments, all the engine pressures, temperatures, and so on were in Doug's location, and I depended on his expertise to advise me when anything looked amiss.

Doug recollected:

I had spent the previous evening in the Sergeants' Mess gambling, and for the first time since my close friend Jimmy's death I was a winner. Jimmy and I had taken engineering training together. Ken came to the mess and told us a mission had been called, and we were bussed to our billets. They awakened us very early in the morning, and we went to briefing. Our crew had made several trips over a short space of time, and I was very tired. I had a boil in my nose, which made wearing my oxygen mask a painful ordeal. I was depressed and wrote a brief letter home, asking that if anything happened to me there should be no bitterness. I gave it to the Padre to mail if I did not return.

Inside, Jim Taylor and Atky double-checked all the pre-flight navigational data to make sure everything was in order. Jim was thorough when it came to exactness in preparing his navigational information. He and Atky made a great pair. Once airborne, Atky assisted him in checking the H2S navigational system to make sure we were not only on course but exactly — and I can say *exactly* — on time all along the way to the target. Using Jim's navigational skills we bombed as close as possible to our programmed time.

Wat made sure the radio equipment was functional and that his supply of radar-jamming foil — "window" — was ready for use. Wat was always available to assist Jim and Atky should the navigational equipment malfunction, requiring a radio fix. Wat also reminded the crew that he was on standby should they need a skilled gunner.

Brock and Curly made sure their turrets and equipment were ready. Brock, from Moose Jaw, Saskatchewan, was one of the quieter members of the crew. Ray, from New Westminster, British Columbia, was always combing his golden blond hair. It was as straight as a board, so we nicknamed him "Curly." Life in the turrets was a lonely existence, and one of my assignments was to call them up from time to time to make sure they were awake. Curly's favorite joke was to ask me, "Do you know what the Indian from the North said to the Indian from the South?"

To which I always replied, "No, what did he say?"

His answer "Hi" was followed by, "Do you know what the Indian from the South said to the Indian from the North?"

Here it comes. "Hi yo'all." This would break him up. But it kept him awake.

Doug and I made the final run-up of our four Hercules-powered engines, and the linkage jammed on our starboard outer engine when I attempted to get maximum rpm's. The jamming froze the starboard throttle and permitted it to open only partially. Under the circumstances, we had to declare the aircraft unserviceable. This was really disturbing to

Brock Folkersen on
the wrong side of his
mid-upper turret.

Jim Taylor at
his navigation
station.

Wat Watson and
Doug Grey, all
ready to go.

Pilot Officer James M. Taylor.

Pilot Officer Darrell "Atky" Atkinson.

Sergeant Ray "Curly" Hughes.

Sergeant Douglas Grey.

Sergeant J. Brock Folkersen.

Sergeant A. A. "Wat" Watson.

me since the aircraft had just come off inspection, and somewhat ironic, too, since the aircraft engines had operated perfectly before they went in for inspection. Superstition began to creep into our thoughts. Was this a bad sign?

There was a mandate that regardless of how the aircraft operated, it went in for inspection according to a fixed schedule. We became concerned because we were eating up the time allotted to get airborne. On some missions if this had happened, a spare crew would have taken our place. For today's mission there were spare aircraft available but not spare crews. We had to get to another aircraft, and quickly. Once a mission was called, to prevent any possible likelihood of interception by the enemy, total radio silence was maintained. We were already under radio silence, and WAG (Wireless Air Gunner) Watson used the Aldis lamp, our only other means of communication, to notify the tower. Shortly a jeep arrived to take us to another aircraft. The officers in the jeep had a diagram of where the spare aircraft were located, and we high-tailed it to one as quickly as possible. We were starting to rush.

With the exception of Doug and me, the Cradle Crew climbed aboard and started the interior check of this new plane. Before we had completed our exterior inspection, Wat "washed out" this kite, for the radio was unserviceable. There was no way we were taking off without serviceable radio equipment.

We were really getting wrought up. Once more superstition reared its ugly head. We went through the same drill, and the jeep picked us up. This time we went to *E.Q.-Queenie*. We were now doing all our checks in double-time. Finally everything checked out and we were ready, all four engines roaring as we headed for the runway in use. When we turned on the runway, we were a few minutes beyond the "last possible minute for takeoff." We half expected a red light from the tower, which would have washed out the operation for us. I felt sure that if this had been a night operation, we would have been given a red light, canceling the trip. No one on our squadron had ever gotten a red light.

We got the green light and roared down the runway, never realizing this would be the last time. Adding to our problems of joining the bombing stream, the runway in use was 180 degrees from our course to the target. This meant that once we were airborne, we would have to double back over the station before setting course.

The time was 6:53 a.m.

Surely all the things that could go wrong had gone wrong. Wrong *again*!

As soon as I took off in *E.Q.-Queenie* I noted the aileron controls were "ropey." When I lifted or dipped the port or starboard wings, they did not respond immediately. Such slow response could be imminently dangerous if we were attacked and I had to perform evasive action. With so many things going wrong, we still did not get the message: "We should have stayed in bed."

If there was to be any chance for us to catch up with the bombing stream it would require flying faster than programmed. This, in turn, would consume more fuel than normal, and I told the crew that they would spend the night in other than their own beds, for we would not have enough fuel to get back to the squadron. Little did I know how prophetic this statement would turn out to be.

The strategy called for a low-level operation, below 2,000 feet, to keep us from being picked up by the German radar defenses until we crossed the German coast. Flying at a higher altitude would have produced a greater airspeed, with the possibility of catching up with the main force.

Our airspeed at 2,000 feet was limited to something better than 160 mph.

When we approached the German coast, the bomber stream was not in sight, and we climbed quickly to 18,300 feet, our designated height for bombing. While we had a seven-man crew, lookouts were limited to Doug Grey, the gunners, and me. We had our eyes peeled, expecting trouble at any moment. We were all alone over enemy territory. There was no protection from being in the middle of the bombing stream. No fighter escort. We kept a particularly close watch for enemy fighters. We were an easy target. On the German radar screens we were a single "blip," easily identifiable. Regardless, no one suggested we turn back.

Based at Germany's Parcnim airfield was the third Staffel (Squadron) of JG-7, flying ME-262s. Armed with 30mm cannon and new R4M rockets, about a dozen fighters from JG-7 were closing in on the Lancasters and Halifaxes.

En route to the target we realized we had used up a lot of petrol, and our plan was to make our bombing run, then head for Belgium. Our fuel would run out on a straight track across the North Sea to our base. We had no idea exactly where we would land at that time.

Finally I could see the bombing stream far ahead of us and hear the master bomber's instructions coming through loud and clear. When we were still some 30 miles away I heard the master bomber say, "OK, gang, let's pack it up."

It had been a long day for them, for they had arrived at the target area well ahead of the bombing stream.

When we heard this we really felt alone. We were too close now to do anything but press on and complete our bombing run. We found out later that the last wave, composed of Six Group, was late, and the fighter cover had begun to withdraw as the bombers approached the target. It was just a few minutes before nine o'clock in the morning.

The first attack appears to have been made on Lancaster "D" of 429 Squadron, piloted by Warrant Officer K. L. Weld, whose aircraft was attacked over the target at 0859 hours. In the next 12 minutes, RCAF bombers reported approximately 50 encounters with the jets. The gunners poured out hundreds of rounds, defending their aircraft and trying to assist other bombers that were under attack. It was a grim battle. Warrant Officer Weld reported that between 0903 and 0905 five Lancasters and one Halifax were seen going down in the target areas. Four Lancs were on fire.

Five parachutes from the other Lanc were seen, and seven from the Halifax.

Lancaster "H" of 429 Squadron was attacked four times by ME-262s, which damaged the upper turret, destroyed the starboard aileron, and left a large hole in the starboard wing. The gunners, Flight Sergeants H. Ross and J. D. Whitehead, directed the pilot, Flying Officer S. F. Avis, in corkscrews, which probably saved them all from destruction. All of this was occurring in front of *E.Q.-Queenie*.

The Pathfinders' sky markers were almost dissolved when we arrived at the target, surprisingly only six minutes late from our programmed time. We proceeded according to plan, using what was left of the markers, together with Jim Taylor's H2S calculations. Cloud cover prevented a visual attack. We made the bombing run as planned.

Moments later, shortly after we had closed the bomb doors and were setting course for home, three ME-262s came out of the sun, and one hit us with his 30mm cannons, across the rear turret. The cone of fire centered on the port wing and set the port outer engine on fire. One minute all was quiet and the next we were hit. I saw two of the ME-262s go under our port wing. We had been told to "Beware of the Hun in the sun." When attacked "down sun" there is not a thing one can do about it. Needless to say, we were all damn scared but had little time to worry.

Chapter 15

Put on Parachutes

*M*Y EYES WERE RIVETED ON the fire in the port outer engine. I had never had to put out a fire before. Would the procedure work? Would the aircraft blow up before we had time to jump? From the hit, our port wing was rolled up like a carpet. I was sure I could never get the aircraft back under reasonably good control. The control column was turned fully to the right with hard right rudder. I applied full aileron rudder trim, yet we were making steep turns to the left. It would be a miracle if I could keep it airborne for another few minutes.

In attempting to put out the fire, I feathered the port outer engine and told the Cradle Crew, "Put on parachutes."

Surprisingly there was little panic. The pilot and tail gunner in a Halifax wear seat parachutes; the balance of the crew wear harnesses, and the parachute unit is stored separately. At the command "Put on parachutes," the parachute unit is removed from where it has been stored and is attached to clips on the chest harness. It would be too awkward to wear the parachute while performing assignments. Everyone proceeded with his role in the abandonment procedure. The responses were magnificent.

Early in the war the command had been "Prepare to abandon aircraft." This was changed to "Put on parachutes." There had been instances where the pilot had given the command "Prepare to abandon aircraft" and due to faulty intercom equipment one or more of the crew had only heard "abandon aircraft." The pilot would subsequently get the aircraft under control only to find out one or more of his crew had jumped. The newer command seemed to correct that situation.

At the command to put on parachutes, Jim Taylor removed the trap door after closing up his navigation table, jettisoned the door hatch, and sat on the floor with his feet sticking out of the hatch opening, awaiting my further command. He later recounted: "I was still plugged in and had my helmet on when the skipper said, 'Jump! Jump!' Off came the helmet and away I went."

Jim was followed by Wat, Atky, Brock, and then Doug Grey.

Curly saw what he thought was a mark on the Perspex glass. The next moment he was staring at three ME-262s. He remembered:

> The hit knocked out three of my four guns, and the one working was no more effective than a peashooter. I told Ken if I had a broom I could have hit them as they went by. I must admit to some panic when I could not operate the doors behind me. Apparently the hit had made the electrical system unworkable. Ken told me to use the axe on the doors, which I did, and I was finally able to manipulate the turret manually. After I took off my flying helmet, I fell backwards out of the turret. Ken insisted on staying until I did. I recall seeing pieces of our wing go by and the rest of the port wing on fire.

Wat, our wireless operator, remembers:

> To the best of my recollection, our late departure prevented

us from ever catching up with the bombing stream, and we arrived late at the target. After dropping our bombs and setting course for our base we were intercepted by two ME-262s. As a wireless operator I am not on the intercom system with the rest of the crew, and do not see or hear what is going on outside the aircraft. While performing my duties at the time, I heard a dull thud, which I imagined was similar to bombs dropping. I realized that at 18,300 feet we were too high to hear bombs dropping, and just at that moment the light on my panel came on, indicating for me to turn on my intercom. On answering the call, I was informed by the pilot that we had taken a hit on our port outer engine, and that he was unable to extinguish the fire. I was ordered to put on my parachute and abandon the aircraft in the normal emergency procedure through the front hatch.

As I recall, the navigator was the first out, then I as wireless operator, followed by the bombardier and the mid-upper gunner, who had come forward from his mid-upper turret. The engineer did all he could to assist the pilot before he was ordered out.

Doug told me later:

We were on fire, and you gave the order to abandon the aircraft, which we did with precision, except for Curly who was unable to get out of his turret immediately. I remember leaving, with you still at the controls waiting for Curly to get out. I almost panicked going through the escape hatch and nearly pulled the ripcord too soon. The sky was overcast. After the chute opened, it seemed to take forever to reach the ground.

Brock Folkersen recalled:

On the command to put on parachutes, the drill called for me to leave my gun turret, attach my chest chute, proceed to the front of the aircraft, and stand adjacent to the pilot and the wireless operator. When I stood beside him, Ken turned and asked me, "Did you bring my skimmer?"

With a smile I said, "If you want your hat you can go and get it for yourself."

Needless to say, my hat went down in flames.
Brock continued:

My first thought was would the chute open and would I clear the aircraft. As close as I can remember, it took some 20 or so minutes for me to descend through the ten-tenths cloud cover.

Meanwhile, inside the aircraft I had my own problems. The Halifax, not responding, continued to fly in a circle. We were rapidly losing height. I made one final call over the intercom to make sure everybody was out. All I got back was the whistling of the wind.

Finally I was all alone in a doomed aircraft, the worst feeling you can imagine. I was wondering, "Did everyone get out all right?" But I did not take long to think about it. I released the seat harness and made a quick leap down over the wireless operator's station to that very small hatch. Would I get out before this kite turned over? I paused over the hatch but only for a moment, thinking, "Damn it! Can I get through that small hole with this seat chute on? Here goes."

Soon I was falling. The ripcord pulled away, and there was a crackling sound. I was afraid to look up, fearing my chute was on fire. On our previous trip I had seen such an event happen to a member of a nearby aircraft. I felt so helpless. Finally I realized I was OK. I looked up at that mess of beautiful silk parachute and said a silent prayer.

Dangling from my harness, I felt suspended in space. My first thought was of the Cradle Crew, which I could see in the distance, strung out like a Monday morning wash. I started counting 1, 2, 3, 4, 5, 6, plus myself — 7; everyone accounted for, thank God.

Jim Taylor recalled his descent:

I didn't seem too frightened. I had always wanted to jump from an aircraft, and I suppose I was a bit excited. My first view after jumping was my open chute above me. I had lost my D ring, and I could see the gaggle of the other kites in the distance. I tried to count the chutes coming from our kite but lost count after four or five. I could also see our port wing, and it looked as if someone had crumpled it up like a newspaper and then tried to straighten it. I heard one of the jets and saw him come at us. He veered off without shooting and headed for the other planes. I can recall seeing the sky-blue underside of the German aircraft and how smooth and sleek it looked. Because we had turned to the left after the run, I was concerned that we might be over water. Actually, at this time we had no idea where we were. I turned myself to face the stream of bombers on their way home and reckoned that was north. I wrapped part of my shroud lines around my arm so that I could drift to the right, easterly, and hoped to alight over land. About halfway down I heard dogs barking and also a rooster crowing. It gave me some relief to know that I was apparently over land.

I saw a clearing in the forest as I approached the ground, and tried to maneuver my chute to drift toward it. I heard gunfire and saw a squad of soldiers in that clearing and decided it was a rifle range. I couldn't determine if they were firing at me or not. If they were, they didn't hit me. As I landed in the clearing it was like sliding into second base. The dead leaves on the ground caused me to slide. When I dumped the air from my chute, ten soldiers approached me. They had crawled through the barbed wire fence and had a revolver pointed at me. I was asked if I had a gun, to which I replied, "No." I was directed to go with the soldiers while one of them took care of my parachute. My watch indicated it was 9:35 a.m. I was in my chute a little over 30 minutes.

When I first saw Doug Grey he had been worked over at the time of his capture. He had numerous cuts and bruises, which together with the fact that he had not shaved in several days made him look even more beaten up.

As second man out, Wat remembers:

The tail gunner after some considerable difficulty was able to exit from the tail turret. There were some heroics that I learned about sometime later. At the time of the attack, the tail turret also took a shell, and half of it was blown off, and the power equipment became unserviceable. The tail gunner had to manipulate the turret manually in order to get out. He was in such difficulty he told the pilot to leave him with the aircraft and save himself. This was not acceptable to our pilot, and he remained with the aircraft until the tail gunner was able to free himself and abandon the aircraft. This action was just another testimonial to the character of our skipper.

After leaving the aircraft through the hatch and pulling the ripcord on the parachute, I evidently passed out from lack of oxygen. After some time I found myself hanging in a chute harness; and feeling nauseous from the oscillation of the harness, I once again lapsed into unconsciousness. When I came to, I was a few hundred feet from the ground. I remember the air being so still and so calm, as it was early morning. At this point I could hear shouts ringing out; evidently I had been sighted, and these were the voices of the German soldiers.

It was my misfortune to land in a tree, and I was knocked unconscious again from striking the tree. When I came to I was sitting on the ground in a wooded area surrounded by German soldiers. I had been searched; they showed me my escape kit and some personal items I had been carrying. I was out of my parachute harness, so I assumed it was still in a tree. The first words I heard were, "The war is over for you" — spoken in English.

Brock later remembered:

When I neared the ground, I could hear sounds coming up to me which seemed strange. Breaking through the low-hanging cloud about 2,000 feet, I was headed for a plowed field, but my descent looked like it would take me into some telephone wires. In grabbing my shroud lines I fell backward into the field; surprisingly it was a soft landing. While I gathered my chute I suddenly heard a voice behind me and turned to see a Reservist, or Home Guard, shaking nervously and pointing a revolver at me. By now others had joined him, including an SS man who asked in English: "Where is your aircraft?"

When I told him I did not know, he and the others escorted me to a building which looked like one of our Manning Depots and placed me in a cell. I had been carrying my chute all the way, and en route I met and passed Wat marching in the center of a group of soldiers. For some reason, my appearance brought out a laugh from Wat.

Wat recalls this incident:

After being extricated from the tree, I was helped to my feet and placed with a platoon of soldiers and led off. While they were taking me to the jail or compound, en route we encountered our mid-upper gunner [Brock Folkersen]. We did our best not to let on we were crew members, but I doubt if we deceived anyone. If it had not been so sad it would have been funny, for in all my life I had never seen a more dejected-looking individual than Brock at that moment. Neither will I forget his appearance. He had the inner lining of his flying suit on, and he was carrying his chute — all bunched up.

The two groups joined together and took Brock and me to the local lock up, where we were placed in separate cells. This was the location where we eventually all assembled, but it was at least two or three days before we knew the fate of the entire crew. We were kept in solitary confinement in small cells with only a wooden bench-like bed. The only time we were permitted out was for interrogation or to go to the bathroom. I cannot remember how many days we spent there, but it was here that we finally learned everyone had gotten out of the aircraft safely.

Doug Grey told me:

I had difficulty collapsing my chute due to the heavy wind, and it was clogged with mud. I couldn't take the time to bury it as recommended. I was close to a heavily wooded area, so I hid my chute in some bushes and dashed for cover. I continued into the woods until I reached a wire fence. There was a mob of civilians on the other side, and when they saw me some of them started shooting. As I had landed in the target area in daylight I fled from them, only to find myself surrounded by a large detachment of soldiers, the Volksturm or Home Guard, to whom I surrendered. One of them had found my chute and had it wrapped around him. I was taken from the soldiers by the civilians. As they attempted to march me past, I was beaten with anything that was handy. If the soldiers had not driven them off I have no doubt that I would have been killed. When they stopped, a squad formed, and an officer marched me out in front of them. The officer drew his revolver and checked the clip. I felt this was the end. I was numb with shock. Then he laughed and told me to sit down while he dismissed the squad. I sat down beside an old soldier. I smoked a pipe at the time and had a tine of sliced plug tobacco. They offered no objection to my smoking. They took me to what looked like a stable, and I was with about 30 others who had been captured at about the same time. No one had anything to smoke. My pipe was passed around like an Indian peace pipe. It was a life saver. I don't recall what happened to the pipe.

We went through interrogation at Pinneberg and then to Hamburg, where we were dragged through the streets in a trailer with people spitting and hurling abuse and anything else that was handy. We were taken to an airport that was so cleverly concealed that it was almost invisible from the ground. The adjoining bunkers contained Russian prisoners, who seemed to be in great pain. We were moved by train to Rostock and then to Barth. I recall vividly all the refugees fleeing from the enemy on both fronts. It seemed like millions of people, mostly women and children and old men. I spoke to a soldier in Rostock who had only one eye. He was on draft, but he did not know where he would be sent. He hoped it would not be to the Eastern front.

Atky — Darrell Atkinson — would never wear his chute harness fastened as tightly as recommended, saying it was uncomfortable. When he bailed out, he quickly found out why it had been recommended to keep the harness tight. The sudden jerk when the chute opened resulted in one or both of the straps between his legs jamming his testicles, and he was out cold immediately. Naturally he had no other recollection of his descent. When he came to they were extricating him from a tree he had landed in, with the German military in command.

Ray (Curly) Hughes remembers that he was able to extricate himself from the tail turret, but says,

> I have no recollection of pulling the rip cord and at first was too frightened to look up at the parachute. My descent was uneventful except to say that I could hear dogs barking and eventually as I got closer to the ground I could hear chickens. I apparently landed on a farm, and when I hit the ground my watch fell off, and I hurt my ankle on the root of a tree. I tried to hide the parachute but gave up on it. I was caught that afternoon by a soldier who wanted to know what I had done with the parachute. I was taken to the Burgemeister, their mayor, who spoke English, and said, "Just remember you were well treated." I had a shave at his house and was finally picked up by a Storm Trooper, who showed me his gun and said, "It's over for you."

While the entire exercise of bailing out was very rapid, the short time sequence was sufficient to spread out the seven of us over quite some distance. Possibly I was slower than the crew in getting out. They told me later they had not seen me leave the aircraft and assumed I had gone in with it.

Ten-tenths — complete — cloud covered the entire area. I wondered if this was a momentary lull before the end. We had just attacked Hamburg, and for all I knew I was descending into a possible blazing inferno from our bombing attack. I could see nothing but cloud. Would there be a firing squad ready to shoot at me as soon as I broke the final cloud layer? Our earlier information was that we had already destroyed four-fifths of industrial Hamburg. There was no way the local inhabitants would be friendly after such an attack. I was scared.

Suddenly I had a strange thought: I wonder which bastard will steal my egg?

An egg! Why should I care who had something as unimportant as an egg? Why wasn't I thinking of my fiancee, my mother, my sister, or brother? No, I am ashamed to admit, my first thoughts were nothing that important. I had to think about an egg.

The day before this trip, Good Friday, a parcel had arrived from my mother containing all my favorite goodies, including a cream-filled Easter egg. I had planned to share the parcel Easter Sunday with the Cradle Crew. The egg was for me.

We had been hit at our bombing altitude of 18,300 feet, and as closely as I could estimate, I had jumped at 11,000 to 12,000 feet. With all I had had to do, I had not spent much time looking at the altimeter.

When the final tally was made for this raid on Hamburg, it was reported that ten bombers and three fighters were missing after the attack. This included five RCAF Lancasters and three RCAF Halifaxes. Allied gunners claimed four ME-262s destroyed, three probably destroyed, and four damaged. There is some speculation that these claims may be too high, but the fact remains that the RCAF put up a gallant fight in that bitter battle over Hamburg.

Unfortunately, *E.Q.-Queenie* was one of the gruesome statistics.

$$\widehat{Chapter\ 16}$$

Capture

W HETHER THE ARMAMENT *was on a fighter plane or a bomber, the guns were all synchronized to create a cone of fire at a given distance. The cone created intense firepower, and if the aircraft was hit in the cone, it would be totally destroyed. While the cone was deadly, it was possible for a fighter to make a hit on a bomber with a portion of his firepower and create sufficient damage that for all intents and purposes it was destroyed. In our particular case, we were not hit by the cone of the ME-262 or none of us would be* alive today. However, the Messerschmitt did damage sufficient to destroy the aircraft.

The Luftwaffe had come out in force and knocked down eight aircraft from Six Group, our largest loss since January 5, when we had lost ten. I do not know how many of the airmen were the whisky-drinking Canadian lumberjacks Lord Haw Haw had referred to. Because of their ages, it was highly unlikely any of them were lumberjacks; but, for sure, most of them were Canadian.

There was no feeling of motion at all during my fall through three layers of cloud. It was almost as if I were hanging in the air — that is, until I broke through the low-hanging stratus around 2,000 feet. The ground appeared to be rushing up at me. I could no longer see any of the crew, and I was thankful there were no fighters shooting at me on the way down. It was generally believed, but not necessarily true, that if one bailed out over enemy territory, the fighters did not waste ammunition and shoot, for the odds were in favor of capture. However, if one was shot down over friendly territory, the enemy might shoot, because once on the ground the crew member would be safe.

We had only simulated a parachute jump in training, but this was the real thing. I had to assume the entire crew would make it safely to the ground. Afterwards they told me that although they had not seen me leave the aircraft, they assumed that if I had been able to bail out, I would be some distance away and the likelihood of joining up with them was remote.

Approaching the ground, I tried to remember everything I had been taught about how to prepare for impact. Everything seemed in order. The chute was drifting downwind and my plan was simple. When I hit, I would roll and break my fall. When I was about 100 feet from the ground I could see two small children, and I felt I was about to crash on top of them. I was being drawn like a magnet in their direction. They were walking along a country road — happy youngsters skipping and throwing rocks at imaginary objects, possibly on their way home. They were totally oblivious to my approaching from above. Alongside the road was an old wooden fence that appeared to have been there for a hundred years. I had two choices: hit the children or hit the fence. I pulled on the shrouds, which took me out of wind, avoiding the children. Instead, I crashed into the old fence, breaking it into pieces.

This was turning into a helluva day.

When the frightened children saw me, they panicked and ran away as fast as their legs could carry them. Their mothers would never believe their story.

My troubles still were not over. My parachute harness jammed. When I hit the release buckle nothing happened. Fortunately I was able to squirm out of it and run for all I was worth for a small forest. I could see people in the distance coming toward me. For all I knew our bombs could have destroyed one or more of their homes, and they would be harder to deal with than the military. I never looked back, so I was unaware if they pursued me. I ran until I was exhausted. It could have been an hour or more.

About this time I fully realized I was a fugitive in an enemy country. To my knowledge none of the crew members, including me, had been injured as a result of being attacked by enemy fighters, or in the process of bailing out of the aircraft. It was reasonable to assume that some, if not all of us, would be captured. Ground forces would find the crashed aircraft, and it would be evident that we had managed to bail out. Cloud cover at the time of the attack provided a minor shield until we broke through the last layer. We had no idea how many would be looking for us, and we had to take great care if we were to make our escape. The circling effect of the aircraft had destroyed any sense of direction we might have had, so we had to be extremely careful in making any decision. Hopefully we would find some signs to help us verify our position.

There must have been a supply of adrenaline in my system that kept me running as long as I did. Memory tells me that our aircraft was hit sometime around nine in the morning, and it was now almost noon. I was awfully tired and had to take a breather. Strange as it may seem, I felt safe for the moment. I was unaware whether I was north, south, east, or west of Hamburg. What I did know was that I was in enemy territory and I had to take care. What were my chances of capture or escape? The odds had to be in favor of capture. Would it be by civilians or military? From my knowledge of the German military I felt it would be better if the military made the capture, for they were disciplined to respect authority, and since I was a flying officer, that should be a plus. On the other hand, if I was real careful I might be able to make my way back to the Allied lines.

While I rested I decided to reduce the chances of recognition. I lowered my trousers over my flying boots and removed my turtleneck sweater. I then pulled it over my battle dress jacket. I decided that with my short blond hair and fair complexion I could pass for a German. I broke open my escape kit and placed the items in different pockets. We had carried these kits on every trip, but until now I had never seen the contents. In one pocket I kept the map — which was all in German, naturally, and not that easy to read. In the other pocket I kept the Horlick tablets, the energy food. The very small compass was enclosed in plastic, and for ready reference I kept it in my fur-lined gloves. We had been informed that if we removed our flying outfit and changed into civilian clothing there was a possibility we would be shot for being a spy. Whether or not that was the case, I did not feel like experimenting.

The day was still cloudy, and while not bitter cold, the air was brisk and damp. I had the feeling that it could start to rain any moment. I noted a lot of signs reading "Verboten" and thought to myself, "This guy sure owns a lot of property." If I got back to England safely I should be able to get a laugh or two with that remark.

The entire area was relatively flat, sprinkled with small wooded areas. I vividly recall seeing bomb craters and wondering if any of these were from the bombs we had dropped. There were several places where the Germans had a reforestation program well under way. They were apparently conscious of the need to replant their natural resources.

This was a part of the war for which we had had no training and had never given much thought. My plan was to head west toward the Allied lines; hopefully I would make contact with the "underground," which would help me escape to England. This thought buoyed my spirits, at least for the moment. Many times that day I started in one direction, then saw a built-up area and reversed my course to avoid it. I seemed to be getting nowhere. Frustration was setting in each time I found it necessary to change direction.

By mid-afternoon I was very tired, so I decided to take a short nap in a grass-lined ditch. When I awoke I could not put any weight on my left foot; it buckled. It looked swollen, and I had to assume that I had sprained it when I had hit the fence. A stick I found served as a cane, and I could walk with difficulty. Nearby I saw workers in a field, undoubtedly bringing in some much needed crop. They either did not see me or did not care. Shortly, I came to a dirt road. I was so thirsty, I realized I would have to find water somewhere. For my lunch I ate a Horlick tablet. I wondered where my next meal would come from.

Buildings in the distance gave me some concern, so I decided to try another route. To my left I saw a forest, which to my mind would be a good place to stay until after dark. To get to it I had to walk along a low hedge and cross over what appeared to be a main highway. I could see a few cars and an occasional bicycle. It had started to rain, and the traffic had almost disappeared. I thought this would be a good time to get started. My foot hurt, but I could manage. It totally amazed me that I had been able to run for over an hour on a sprained ankle — one effect of shock.

As I came to the road, I saw that it curved to my left; I could not see beyond. No sooner had I started to cross the road than around the bend came a German officer — an oberleutnant — and a sergeant, both riding bicycles directly toward me. I saw a Luger revolver on the belt of the sergeant. Doubtless the officer also carried small arms under his greatcoat. I was frightened. There was no way I could run with a sprained ankle. Our Intelligence officers had said, "When you have no other alternative, try bluffing." I had no choice but to try it: keep cool and look unconcerned.

I started to swing my "cane" as I walked toward them. I nodded as I passed, and kept on walking. My foot was really hurting. I tried to walk in a normal manner, and I did not dare use the cane. My breathing was undoubtedly labored, for at any moment I expected to hear a gunshot that would end it all. Still I did not panic, but just kept walking, slowly. I dared not look back. With each step I began to feel my bluff was more successful. Suddenly I saw a bicycle tire at my side. The two Germans had returned. Now I had to stop. They said something to me. Obviously they still did not realize I was anything but German. The lieutenant spoke to me, and I did not have a clue what he was saying. I hoped he was simply asking for a cigarette, so I checked my pockets and shrugged. Then he said, "English?"

I nodded. Was this the end?

With this, he pulled out a small Mauser automatic from under his greatcoat and stepped back. I believe that at the outset he was more afraid of me with my stick than I was of him with his gun. I was sure it was all over, and I told myself to forget the cream-filled Easter egg. While the officer held the gun, the sergeant searched me. When he found I had no weapons, he commandeered a passing truck, and we were driven to that area that I had decided to avoid earlier. My intuition had been right on, for the buildings I had seen in the distance on the dirt road were a small German military camp. On the way he castigated me as a "killer of innocent women and children."

I had felt sure he would shoot me on that lonely road in the rain, but maybe his ego was better satisfied by bringing me in and reveling on his skills at having captured me. He undoubtedly embellished the story at every telling as to how clever he had been in making the catch. On the other hand, maybe he was saving me for a firing squad. Lots of thoughts ran through my mind, and I can assure you none of them were pleasant. The weather did not help. It was cold, and the drizzle had turned into a downpour.

Inside the office all my personal effects, dog tags, and the contents of the escape kit were documented, plus one other item — a partial package of Wrigley's Juicy Fruit Gum. All British air crews when on a mission were ordered never to carry any personal items such as snapshots or mementos, which might be used by the Germans against them if they were captured. By this time I felt that at least for the moment, they were not going to shoot me.

The office I was in might have been identical to one at our base, except that the lone picture on the wall was one of Adolf Hitler. While I sat on a table anxiously listening to the Germans discuss my capture, two things took on an amusing aspect. Strange the way the mind works — I expected to be shot at any moment and instead found something amusing. It was interesting that while I did not understand a word either of the Germans said, their body language told the story. When the corporal who did the documenting got to the gum, he obviously did not know what it was. He held it in his hand and asked the oberleutnant. The oberleutnant, not wanting to appear stupid to a lowly corporal, picked up the package, stared at it, and then in a loud voice tried to pronounce and translate two words that were very difficult to say in German. It sounded to me like he said, "Oosy Fruitenbaum."

Serious as the situation was, I could not help laughing. They both gave me a dirty look as the corporal went back to cataloguing my belongings. To this day, every time I see or chew a piece of Wrigley's Juicy Fruit Gum, I have to smile. At the time it might have made a good commercial.

The second incident concerned my compass, which was about the size of my little finger nail. Continuous usage during the day dictated that I keep it in the fur-lined gloves, but annoyingly it would work its way into the fingers. It was somewhat difficult to remove from the long fur-lined fingers, and basically it had been a damn nuisance.

My gloves were lying on a table in the oberleutnant's office, and when I had removed them the compass had once again found its way into a finger. It would be interesting to see, I thought, whether or not they would find it. I certainly was in no position to use it. Finally I was told to put on the clothes they had removed. Possibly I was in too much of a hurry to put on the gloves, when suddenly the officer grabbed them. After turning them inside out, he found the compass.

Glory hallelujah! He was absolutely overjoyed with his discovery. Surely I did not think I could put something over on him? This was doubly amusing, because unknown to him, we also wore a compass as a button on our shoulder epaulet. When this was first tried, the epaulet compass, which looked like an ordinary button, unscrewed counterclockwise. The Germans soon discovered the compass and how it worked. The Intelligence unit reversed the thread on the screw, fooling the Germans for a while before they discovered the change. Intelligence then put the thread back the way it had been originally, and to my knowledge the Germans never became aware of the second change. They did not think we would be that stupid.

After loading me into a small truck, they drove into Hamburg to several different military installations. By this time the rain had stopped, but the skies were still very overcast. At each stop, my officer "friend" had to describe to all who would listen how clever he was in discovering the compass. At every stop he would do the "Heil Hitler!" salute, both on arrival and on departure. He then would go into what I assumed was great detail and dramatic gesturing in finding the compass. He no doubt thought he was a candidate for the German Iron Cross. Once again, although I could not understand one word he was saying, I was completely aware of the story he told them.

Hamburg was in a shambles from Allied bombing. From what I was able to observe, the estimate of four-fifths of the city destroyed did not seem unreasonable. Only the residential areas were intact. The Allies felt that it would take over five years to clear the rubble from the bombed-out areas. The people who lived and worked there went about their business with hardly a glance at me.

My German lieutenant cared little about the city. He had made a valuable capture and discovery. I was not handcuffed, but with the gun my

officer friend was wearing and my sore ankle, there was not much likelihood that I would have been able to escape. When I looked at my watch,
I realized that it had been seven hours since I had been captured.

At the end of the day, the lieutenant put me in a cell at Pinneberg, which
he referred to as "Dulag Luft." The following day I was put in another
Dulag Luft location with all the recently captured prisoners. Needless to
say, I was delighted to find all my Cradle Crew alive and well. I signaled
them not to recognize me, because this might be helpful when we were
being interrogated, which I felt sure would be very soon. When we finally
had a chance to talk, Doug Grey, smoking a cigarette he had found somewhere, said in his wry way, "What kept you?"

At interrogation, I gave them my name, rank, and serial number in
response to their several questions. I wondered if they would accept this or
whether they would try some other tactics to make me give them information they desired. The questions continued and my answers were the same.
Between questions, my interrogator would make some observations in the
hope that I would bite on the comment and make a statement. One of the
observations was that it was difficult for them to comprehend that both
Lancasters and Halifaxes were utilized on the same mission. My response
was a shrug of the shoulders. I was surprised by one question that tried to
tie me in with some of the other prisoners. I let it stand. Apparently my
signal to the crew when I first saw them had not been picked up by the
Germans. They were surprised I could speak only English. They let me
know that all the officers in the Luftwaffe were able to speak several lan-
guages. That was my one and only interrogation.

Jim Taylor remembered his interrogation:

> I was questioned at various times of the day. I had never felt
> as chilled, damp, and miserable as I did when I sat in the inter-
> rogation room. It was raining, and I always seemed to be sched-
> uled to walk to interrogation in the rain. My clothes never did
> get dry. I was amazed that the interrogation officer knew what
> squadron I was from. Apparently Atky had a slip of paper in his
> battle dress with our Gee coordinates on it. He had misplaced it
> just the week before when we were out on practice bombing
> runs. He hadn't realized it was in his pocket, and the Germans
> found it. The officer showed me pictures of our squadron taken
> from the air. One of their favorite ploys was to name some of

the members of the crew and entice you to name the rest. It did not work, but they seemed to know that Atky, Brock, and I were from the same crew.

They may not have pressed this point because it had to be a rarity for the entire crew of a bomber to have escaped from its aircraft when the plane was shot down.

We were placed in separate cells during this part of our stay. Doors would open and close, and I was unable to tell what was happening. It was a frightening experience. For all I knew they could be taking us out and shooting us one at a time. The room was very small, with a single cot and a stool. I could not eat the German food. I had never drunk coffee in my life, and I was not about to start on the green version they served us. The cell door opened, and the guard brought me a terrible tasting sandwich. I had always been a fussy eater. I told the guard to put the sandwich on the small stool, the only piece of furniture in the room other than the bunk. The sandwiches soon piled up, but I continued to chew the now tasteless piece of Wrigleys Juicy Fruit Gum I had been chewing when I was shot down. At night I would stick the gum behind my ear and pull it off in the morning and say to myself, "Here's breakfast."

They did not permit us to talk through the walls, and the only conversation I had was when I would call out "vasser," meaning "water," and "piss," which was self evident. While I knew the word for eating was "essen," I did not use it, for I was not taken with their food. When I called out, the guard would open the door and take me to the toilet, where I could take care of my needs. I was considerably concerned about knowing what was happening to the rest of the crew, so I devised a means of determining whether we were still all intact.

At the station we had often gone out together, and we had a favorite musical riff. There were no words that we knew of, so we would "sing" the tune together. Later, Count Basie developed this riff into an instrumental number called "Feeding the Bean." I decided to use it for a musical roll call. Because there were no words, I felt the Germans would not realize what we were doing. After singing the first line I waited, and soon I heard the second progression, the third, and so on, until all the crew members had "reported" in. This was done every few hours, and the Germans never caught on to what we were doing. It gave me a great deal of comfort to know that everyone was all right. I was sure they felt the same.

Finally, on April 4, some 30 of us were brought together into one room. This was the first time we had actually seen the other prisoners who had been with us in the Dulag Luft. Surprisingly most of them were quite upbeat; their main complaint was the lousy food. After about an hour, an oberleutnant entered the room and in very clear, concise English gave us the following options: "We can continue to keep you here in the Dulag Luft with the same limited amount of food available to you, or we can move you to a prison camp where you will have access to Red Cross parcels and considerably better living conditions. We do not have suffi-cient guards to supervise such a transfer. There are some 30 of you, and we can only provide 2 guards to handle this assignment. We have decided for you that you are going to the camp. The guards have been instructed that should any attempt be made to escape, the American captain, the senior officer among you, will be shot on the spot."

It appeared they had resolved the problem. I am sure the American cap-tain was not too comfortable with the arrangement, for he could not be assured one of the other nationalities might not attempt an escape.

That same day, we started out from Hamburg by train and witnessed the flight of the refugees from both fronts. Most of them were being moved in boxcars, desperately hanging onto those personal possessions they held dear. They looked terribly frightened. Some of them may have been on their way to one of the death camps.

Our own fears were still with us, for we had no idea what life would be like in the prison camp. We changed trains at Rostock, which was crowded with troops waiting to go to the fronts. The guards herded us off to one side near a lumber yard, where we waited for a passenger train connection.

In the midst of this sad scene, a humorous experience (or so I thought) took place. I was still on my Wrigleys Juicy Fruit Gum diet, and the gum was turning to stone. My ear was getting sore where I stuck it every night. I was really hungry. Atky and I noticed workers unloading freight cars. Prior to enlisting I had worked for a railroad. Possibly this made me more aware of the German railroad equipment. The actions of the guards was very loose, to say the least. No doubt this was driven by the fact that they had authority to shoot our group captain if anyone tried to run. It had started to rain, and the railroad workers began leaving the area, so Atky and I decided to see what was in the freight cars. We hoped to find some kind of food. We entered the first car and found a can of jam. I had pil-fered a glass along the way and kept it in my battle tunic. Using the glass,

I scooped up some jam from the tin and replaced the lid. I covered the glass with some paper off the tin. With this initial success, we concluded there must be some real food inside the boxcar. Atky guarded the door in case the workers returned, while I inspected the boxes for more substantial food. I drove my fist through one box and found the hardest biscuits I had ever eaten in my life. For all I knew they may have been dog biscuits. These biscuits will be OK with jam, I thought, as I filled my tunic with a goodly supply.

"They're coming back!" Atky called out, and we quickly left the boxcar.

The guards gave us some strange looks when we returned. I was beginning to have some second thoughts that they might decide to shoot me for stealing. I went behind a lumber pile and transferred quite a few of the cookies into one of my pant legs, then gave up as our train connection approached. Word had spread among the other prisoners, and they wanted me to share my loot. I told them to wait until we were on board.

The train was similar to the British type — the compartments could only be entered from each side. Once the train was moving, passengers were confined to being with those in the compartment. When we pulled out of the station, "George," our name for one of the guards, boarded our compartment and sat opposite me. Just my luck. I began to wonder whether the guards suspected something when they saw me get into the first coach. He seemed to be staring at me too much. I never did like the look of the rifle he wore. I figured, "There goes lunch. Oh, what the hell; maybe he's hungry too."

Everyone in the compartment was wondering how I was going to handle the situation. I did not keep them in suspense for long. I reached into my tunic and slowly pulled out a cookie and offered it to George. He grabbed it so quickly he momentarily caught me off balance. He apparently did not care where I had gotten it.

"We're in, gang!" I said. Without hesitation, I passed the cookies around to the others. "If you think he was surprised with the first one, wait until you see the look on his face when I put jam on the next one."

Some of the guys in the compartment were knocking themselves out watching this Abbott and Costello routine. Apparently the first cookie hit the spot, and George grabbed the second one even faster than the first.

"I wonder what kind of reaction I'll get from him when I reach inside my pant leg for the next round. Here goes."

The look on his face this time was one of total amazement. He had to wonder what the hell I was up to when I started to unzip my trousers, reach in, and pull out the last batch of cookies.

The rest of the trip to Barth was uneventful except for one minor incident. It was interesting to watch the guards smoke a German cigarette. When they got down to what we would call a butt, they would hold the cigarette with a straight pin and smoke it down to the very end. When a German smoked a cigarette there were no butts.

On April 5 we arrived at the little town of Barth, in Pomerania, on the Baltic Sea, where we were unloaded from the train and put into trucks for our short journey to Stalag Luft 1.

On April 3, at 3:06 p.m., the Royal Canadian Air Force at Ottawa, Ontario, sent my mother the following telegram:

REGRET TO ADVISE THAT YOUR SON FLYING OFFI-CER KENNETH KEANE BLYTH J-THREE NINE SIX TWO SEVEN IS REPORTED MISSING AFTER AIR OPERA-TIONS OVERSEAS MARCH THIRTY FIRST STOP LET-TER FOLLOWS —

RCAF CASUALTIES OFFICER.

It was delivered to my mother by a Canadian Pacific Telegraph boy who arrived at her door on a bicycle. My mother had always been fearful of telegrams, and this one was no exception. She asked, "Is it bad news?"

"It could be worse," he replied, and quickly went back to his bicycle. In the mail she received a two-page letter dated April 3, 1945, from Wing Commander F. R. Sharpe, the commanding officer of 408 Squadron.

By this time my mother had been a widow for 11 years. What was she to do? I was the breadwinner of the family, and terrible thoughts of what might have happened to me would not leave her mind.

She wept.

My sister Nancy and my brother George did their best to comfort her. I believe the stress of this event helped bring about her death two years later.

In Saskatoon, my wife-to-be received the following telegram from my mother:

RECEIVED WORD KEN IS MISSING IN ACTION, STILL
LOTS OF HOPE
                                        MARGARET BLYTH

Something Sarah had feared would happen had happened. In an upstairs room, sitting alone by a window, looking at the stars in the darkness, she prayed. She felt a closeness to God in praying that I would be safe. We know many loved ones and friends prayed for every crew member. They were all left in this traumatic state from April 3 until May 21. No word reached them that we were prisoners of war.

On May 21, the prayers of my mother, family, and Sarah were answered. The following letter arrived from RCAF Headquarters in Ottawa:

Confirming my telegram of recent date, I am pleased to inform you that the Royal Canadian Air Force Casualties Officer, Overseas, has advised me that your son, Flying Officer Kenneth Keane Blyth, previously reported missing, is now reported to have arrived safely in the United Kingdom, on May 12th, 1945.

Chapter 17

At Last — Release

*T*HE GERMAN GUARDS *at Stalag Luft 1, most of whom spoke and understood English, were quite friendly. The mood was passive; they appeared to believe they were winning the war. As part of their daily routine they would undoubtedly check the large map of what we called the European Theater of Operations. The slight adjustments made from time to time showing the Allies closing in had to discourage them. Little did they know that the situation was even more critical than that shown on the open map; but they had no reason to believe that it was inaccurate. We knew, however, from the BBC news broadcasts that the map was not being kept current.*

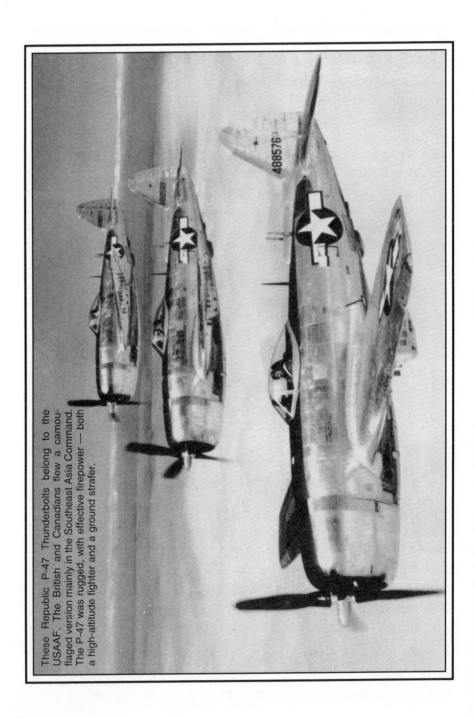

These Republic P-47 Thunderbolts belong to the USAAF. The British and Canadians flew a camouflaged version mainly in the Southeast Asia Command. The P-47 was rugged, with effective firepower — both a high-altitude fighter and a ground strafer.

We theorized that the senior German officers were well aware of the true state of the war. At approximately 1:00 a.m. on April 30, 1945, the Camp Kommandant, Oberst von Warnstedt, informed U.S. Army Air Forces Colonel Hubert Zemke and Royal Air Force Group Captain Cecil Weir, the two senior Allied officers, that the Germans were evacuating the camp, leaving the Allied officers in charge. Upon awaking that morning the Kriegies found that the German guards had been replaced by American POWs, fully armed, wearing MP armbands. These military police were instructed to keep order and discipline.

I later learned that at one time von Warnstedt had demanded that the entire camp be moved westward on foot some 150 miles. Colonel Zemke and Group Captain Weir had steadfastly refused. Obviously, von Warnstedt realized that with his limited force he could not move 9,000 men unless their senior officers were willing to direct them to do so. Their fear of the approaching Russian forces convinced them they should move their German detachment out of the area as quickly as possible.

At the same time as their departure, the Germans at the Flak School felt it wise to leave the area. We could hear explosions coming from the school; they destroyed any equipment they felt would be useful to the Russians. The girls in training on the radar instruments were being evacuated. We could see them packing and moving out.

Later, the world would learn that Adolf Hitler had committed suicide on April 30, 1945, in his bunker at the Reichschancellery in Berlin.

Colonel Zemke became the camp's commanding officer, assisted by Group Captain Weir. Because the majority of the prisoners were American, it was only proper that Colonel Zemke should be in command. Prior to being captured, he had commanded the 56th Fighter Group, dubbed the "Zemke Wolfpack," which recorded 667 air triumphs. Colonel Zemke was personally responsible for 17 aerial victories and 11 ground victories. The 56th flew P-47 Thunderbolts as part of the 8th Air Force Fighter Command. Colonel Zemke's honors included a Silver Star, Purple Heart, Distinguished Flying Cross, Air Medal, and Legion of Merit. He had crashed in late 1944 and had been captured and made a prisoner in Stalag Luft 1.

At Stalag Luft 1, the senior Allied officers had been located in sparse quarters in North 1. Their organization was known as Provisional Wing X. However, with the departure of the Germans, they moved into the Luftwaffe Administration Building in the west compound. Needless to say, the quarters were pure luxury compared to what they had had in North 1.

One of Colonel Zemke's first actions was to assign a military detachment to transport the Red Cross parcels from the Flak School back inside the camp. His concern, subsequently justified, was that the German people might learn of their location and attempt to steal them; attempts to break into the Flak School already had been made. There were 50,000 parcels in storage at the time of the Germans' departure, enough to feed the camp for slightly better than five weeks.

Another early action was to provide popular music over the camp's loudspeaker system. With the daily uncertainty as to what would happen next, this did a great deal to ease the tension.

We found ourselves to be an Allied island surrounded by the enemy. The Allied commanding officers decided we could not sit and wait to be rescued by either our own forces or the Russians, though they agreed that the Russian lines were closer, and an attempt should be made to contact them. A reconnaissance patrol was formed — made up of an American major, a British officer who spoke German, and an American officer who spoke Russian. They set out in an automobile that had an American flag draped over one fender and a white flag on the other. They were headed toward Barth, then on to the Stralsund-Rostock road to await the arrival of the Russian frontline troops.

George, our friendly guard, returned on his bicycle, saying, "I've decided to take my chances with you people." We never did learn what happened to him. He may have returned to a farm in South Saskatchewan!

On May 2 our search party found and brought back First Lieutenant Alec Nick Karmyzoff, infantryman from Tula, Russia. I was near the front gate when he arrived on horseback and, without dismounting, rode his horse through the high entrance in the office building being used by our camp commanders, Zemke and Weir. He held Colonel Zemke at gunpoint. It was a frightening experience; he made it abundantly clear who he thought was in charge at that particular moment. Beside him, also on horseback, was his girlfriend-companion. In his drunken stupor he was insisting that we take down all the barbed-wire entanglements. With some smooth talking the colonel was eventually able to calm the Russian lieutenant. The Germans had left a small liquor supply, and after a few Schnapps a friendlier atmosphere prevailed. The Russian officer learned where the Russian compound was located within the camp and paid it a visit.

We were elated to know that we had been rescued by the Russians, but we were not clear as to what this would mean concerning our departure for England. In the next few days, when more of the Russians appeared in the area, we heard some grim tales of the Cossacks looting and raping the German women. Under such circumstances most of us were quite content to stay inside the compound.

At this point all camp activity ceased. No more baseball or soccer games. No talent shows by the Kriegies. But to our surprise, a traveling troupe of Russian dancers came to the camp and put on a great show. They were part of a professional organization, and their singing and dancing was the best entertainment any of us had seen for a considerable time. Food parcels started to pile up. We ate just enough to keep us going — food that took little or no preparation. Time was now really heavy on our hands.

Though we were "free," the American MPs manned the posten towers and kept a reasonable measure of control for our own safety. Surprisingly, they did not prevent us from leaving the compound, so some of the men ventured out to the deserted Flak School, bringing back all kinds of souvenirs: parts of military uniforms, swastikas, and even German Lugers, the favorite sidearms of the German military officers. Moon Mullen, Mac, and Lee went off looting and found a liquor barge on an inlet on the Baltic Sea. The barge was within walking distance of the camp, and all three came back well in the bag. They had traded off soap for eggs and chicken. Moon was holding a dead chicken by the neck; he wanted it cooked up for supper. I do not remember whether we ate it, but chances are we did.

Most of us were content to visit some of the other compounds in the hope we might locate an old friend. The day I went, I was unsuccessful, but it was interesting to find those POWs also trying to amuse themselves to keep from going berserk during the long wait to get out of the camp. Later that same day Brock and I went for a walk along the Baltic Sea coast. We found an abandoned rowboat and took a short boat ride.

On May 5, Russian Marshal Konstantin Rokossovsky visited the camp. He was disturbed to find only the senior officers wearing black arm bands out of respect for the death of American President Franklin D. Roosevelt. The BBC news of April 12 had announced the death of the President, and most of the senior Allied officers attempted to wear a black arm band. Overall there was no effort to do so. The Germans must have been driven wild wondering how we knew of the President's death before they had received such information.

Rokossovsky was in command of the 2nd Belorussian Front, with the major purpose of clearing out all the Germans from southern East Prussia, northern Poland, Pomerania, and Mecklenburg. It is interesting to note that this was the same Marshal Rokossovsky who met with British Field Marshal Bernard L. Montgomery in the seaside town of Wismar to celebrate the German surrender.

Chapter 18

Homeward Bound

AY 8, 1945 — V-E DAY — we had hoped to be back in England. We heard all kinds of rumors, but, still no action. One moment a Kriegie would come around with the latest "pucka gen" — authoritative information — that we would be marching out to some unknown location. Then we would hear that the Russians were going to fly us out — again to some unknown destination — apparently "duff gen," not worth a damn. However, we were so anxious to get out of the camp, we were ready to latch on to any rumor that sounded reasonable to us at the time.

Finally, over the camp closed-circuit radio we were told that General Dwight D. Eisenhower would have a message for all POWs, which got everyone excited. Quiet reigned as we stood listening for his words of encouragement. The total message: "All POWs, stand by." That was it?!

Everyone was dumbstruck. Where in hell did he think we were going? We let off some of our frenzy by starting a big fire in the center of the parade square, using two of the guard houses for kindling.

We had to be concerned about our health. With the departure of the Germans, we lost the equipment to empty the outhouses — the 50-seaters. These buildings had to be completely sealed off. It now became necessary to dig slit trenches in remote areas of the compound and hang our tails over a makeshift crossbar arrangement to do our daily b.m.'s. The trenches had to be filled in daily, and finding a work detail became a problem. We were greatly disturbed. If we did not leave the camp soon, some form of major illness could easily break out.

In checking the Barth airfield to determine its ability to handle a large force of aircraft for the air evacuation, one of our reconnaissance groups found a concentration camp for Greek and French civilian prisoners. The barbed-wire entanglements were electrified. About 2,000 emaciated prisoners were doing forced labor. Some were taken back to our camp hospital for treatment, but they were too far gone, and they eventually died. Others were dead in their barracks. They had been slowly starved to death. The Russians attempted to assist those remaining, but with rather limited success.

May 12, 1945 — at last the day had arrived. Once again the rumor mill started spewing out the weird stories of how we were going to be evacuated. At this point we really did not care how it was done. We were practically convinced that they would march us out to some specified location, when suddenly we were informed that aircraft were en route to fly us out.

British Field Marshal Montgomery had cleared the air evacuation with Marshal Rokossovsky. Aircrew officers were used to direct and take charge of non-aircrew POWs because many, if not all, had never been in an airplane. We were loaded into lorries and taken to the airfield, which was not far from our camp. The B-17 Flying Fortresses and C-47 Skytrains had been stripped of all armament before arriving. We had no luggage; the only items we took out of the camp were ones we could carry. We were quickly loaded aboard a B-17 around 4:00 p.m.; we took off at 5:50 p.m. to head for England.

The B-17G Flying Fortress, such as the one shown here of the USAAF, was flown by Canadians in a Coastal Command role painted white with sea-gray upper surfaces.

I was placed in charge of 25 Britishers, who had been in the camp since the evacuation of Dunkirk, in May-June 1940! They were so demoralized they no longer cared when they would get back to England. They sat huddled together, and when the pilot flew low over some of the heavily bombed-out areas on the way, which was interesting to me, the Britishers showed little or no interest.

When we neared the coast of England I was invited to sit in the copilot seat of the B-17. I just had to kid the pilot. It was getting dark, and I asked him if he planned to fly around until the sun came up. He gave me a quizzical look. He knew I was referring to the fact that the American forces flew mostly daylight raids, whereas the Canadian and British crews usually flew at night.

On our landing approach, he turned on his landing lights. I had to stick him again: "Can't see where you're going, eh?"

He just gave me a dirty look and turned them off. The British and Canadian forces did not use landing lights, for we had found there were cases where German night fighters stayed with the bombing stream on its return from a mission. If the aircraft turned on their landing lights, they were sitting ducks for these fighters — rather ironic to fly nine hours on a mission, about half over enemy territory, to bomb the target, and then upon return to be shot down in one's own circuit.

By this time my pilot friend was getting a little cheesed off with all this kidding, but he took it pretty well. He greased the aircraft to a perfect landing. I had to give him one more shot, because he had looked at me, expecting some congratulations for a super landing: "With a minimum of training we could use you in the RCAF."

"You're rotten," he replied with a smile on his face. I was surprised he did not let me have it after that remark.

What a feeling of relief to be back in England! The following day we were moved by train to Bournemouth for eventual repatriation to Canada. This was *deja vu*. Prior to the war, Bournemouth had been one of the most beautiful vacation resort centers in England. And once again we were billeted in the many hotels in downtown Bournemouth. We could only imagine how elegant they had been prior to the war. We felt sure they would be restored once it was over. Typically the English are prone to restore rather than rebuild.

It was presumed, and possibly rightly so, that because we had spent various lengths of time as POWs we were undernourished. Large quantities of fresh fruit were shipped from the U.S. and made available to us, particularly oranges. A number of young English boys hung around outside our canteens to beg for oranges. Throughout six years of war, probably no one had been able to find an orange in all of England, and these youngsters could not get their fill. One of them approached me asking for oranges; his mouth, almost up to his nose, was an orange color, so I asked him how many he had already eaten. "I've had six and me chum has had seven."

No doubt both their parents would wonder what they had gotten into that day when they spent all night running to the toilet.

Before we left Bournemouth, all our noncommissioned officers were promoted to pilot officers. This was as it should be. In fact, they should have been officers from the day we became an official crew. Atky, Jim, and I were very happy for them.

One of my buddies who had graduated with me at Service Flying Training School, in Saskatoon, and had received his wings at the same ceremony, was Derrick "Red" Mettrick. Though we had graduated on the twin-engine Cessna Crane, Red was disappointed he had not had the good fortune to receive his wings on single-engine aircraft. He had aspirations of becoming a famous fighter pilot. Fate had other plans, and like me he ended up flying bombers. Red made one second dickie trip, and since the next mission was a daylight raid, he was able to take his crew. The following mission was a night mission, and he was required to go along, once again, as a second dickie pilot. Lo and behold, the aircraft was shot down. Red ended up in a prison camp, and that was the end of his flying in World War II. You can be sure the crew he flew with believed he had jinxed them.

I met Red again in Bournemouth. He apparently had already decided that he would be a commercial pilot once he returned home. He applied to and was accepted by KLM airlines. He obviously had the necessary skills, because he

Fred "TF" Davey, Dirk "Red" Mettrick, Ken Blyth, and Bill Brennan.

made it through their difficult training program and became a successful pilot. By now, no doubt, he is enjoying his retirement.

June 10, 1945, we were loaded aboard the *Ile de France* and returned to Canada. In typical RCAF fashion, immediately after docking in Halifax, we had to muster for a parade inspection. The RCAF does not permit the wearing of any decoration on a dress uniform, unless the decoration has been approved by RCAF Headquarters. Regardless, I decided I would wear my parachute and wings pin made for me by one of the Kriegies. The Air Commodore doing the inspecting was hurrying along, as they usually do. He had gotten about two steps past me when he stopped in his tracks and returned to ask about the pin. I told him that it had been made in the prison camp.

"Wonderful." He kept on walking.

Back at Barth

*J*N THE EXCITEMENT *of the German authorities depart-*
ing on May 1, leaving Stalag Luft 1 in our charge, there
had been a dramatic change in the attitude of all the
POWs. Our daily routine had stopped almost immedi-
ately, and everyone sat around, waiting for something to happen.
Rumors spread daily as to when we would be released. We all
knew that Major Braithwaite and Sergeant Korson, our Stalag
scouts, had gone out in search of the Russian lines. This was a
particularly dangerous assignment, because they were roam-
ing in enemy territory and the Russians had a penchant at this

particular time for shooting at anything they did not think was their own.

Our scouts were successful. To advise the camp of what they had found, on Saturday, May 5, they had the *Barth Hard Times* printed. In the euphoria of the moment, it never occurred to any of us to question how this had been accomplished. I am sure they did not just slide into Barth, find a local printer, and have him produce this edition. We still do not know.

The following are from the *Barth Hard Times* editors.

BARTH HARD TIMES

Vol 1   No. 1   LAST 1   SATURDAY MAY 5th 1945
PRICE 1 D- BAR
Editor: F/L E. R. INKPEN   Assoc: 1st Lt. N. GIDDINGS
Publisher: 1st Lt. D. MacDONALD
Printing: F/LT J. D. WHITE

RUSSKY COME!

As seen by LOWELL BENNET, I.N.S. War Correspondent.

RELIEVED!

Colonel Zemke intended to write this appreciation of the relief of Stalag Luft 1, but unfortunately necessary duties have made this impossible. He has, in his own words, "taken a powder" to make final arrangements with the relieving Soviet forces.

It is therefore my privilege to introduce this Memorial Edition of the BARTH HARD TIMES.

During the successes, reverses and stagnant periods encountered during this struggle, our newspaper has faithfully recorded the German war communiques and expanded upon them in capable editorials.

With the redemption of a continent, our exile is ended. Our barb-bound community will soon be a memory. So, on behalf of Colonel Hubert Zemke and myself, to all our fellow-kriegies: G O O D L U C K!

G./C. C. T. Weir.

BARTH

HARD TIMES

Vol 1   No. 1   LAST 1   SATURDAY MAY 5th 1945   PRICE 1 D- BAR

Editor: FLT E. R. INKPEN   Assoc: 1st Lt N. GIDDINGS   Publisher: 1st Lt D. MacDONALD   Printing: FLT J. D. WHITE

RUSSKY COME!

RELIEVED!

As seen by LOWELL BENNET, I, N. S. War Correspondent.

Colonel Zemke intended to write this appreciation of the relief of Stalag Luft I, but unfortunately necessary duties have made this impossible. He has, in his own words, "taken a powder" to make final arrangements with the relieving Soviet forces.

It is therefore my privilege to introduce this Memorial Edition of the BARTH HARD TIMES. During the successes, reverses and stagnant periods encountered during this struggle, our newspaper has faithfully recorded the German war communiques and expanded upon them in capable editorials.

With the redemption of a continent, our exile is ended. Our barb-bound community will soon be a memory. So, on behalf of Colonel Hubert Zemke and myself, to all our fellow kriegies: G O O D L U C K !

G. C. C. T. Weir.

WHAT DYE KNOW- JOE!!

BRAITHWAITE FINDS UNCLE JOE

Contacts Russian Infantryman at Crossroads
Five miles South of Stalag One.

Major Braithwaite and Sgt Korson, our Stalag scouts, raced out to a cross-roads 5 miles south of Barth with the order, "find Uncle Joe". This was 8 p. m., May 1.

They searched southward, defying a rumored Russian curfew which was about as brief and emphatic as their own order: "EVERYONE stay put; anyone seen moving will be shot on sight"

Meanwhile, Wing Commander Backburn's telephone crew were ringing numbers in Stralsund, hoping a Russan would answer the phone and we could break the big news of our presence. "Try the mayor," they asked the girl (who was still working Barth's phone exchange). "Not a chance," said she. "Barth's mayor poisoned himself and Stralsund's mayor has sprouted wings."

Scouts Braithwaite and Korson pushed on 3 miles. The scenery: thousands of people everywhere, sitting down, waiting.

BRAITHWAITE FINDS UNCLE JOE
Contacts Russian Infantryman at Crossroads
Five miles South of Stalag One.

Major Braithwaite and Sgt Korson, our Stalag scouts, raced out to a cross-roads 5 miles south of Barth with the order, "find Uncle Joe". This was 8 p.m., May 1.

They searched southward, defying a rumored Russian curfew which was about as brief and emphatic as their own order: "EVERYONE stay put; anyone seen moving will be shot on sight."

Meanwhile, Wing Commander Blackburn's telephone crew were ringing numbers in Stralsund, hoping a Russian would answer the phone and we could break the big news of our presence. "Try the mayor," they asked the girl (who was still working Barth's phone exchange). "Not a chance," said she. "Barth's mayor poisoned himself and Stralsund's mayor has sprouted wings."

Scouts Braithwaite and Korson pushed on 3 miles. The scenery: thousands of people everywhere, sitting down, waiting. Every house draped with red flags (who said the Germans weren't chameleons?). Suddenly, there was Uncle Joe — or one of his ambassadors: a chunky little Dead End guy who zoomed up and flashed a variety of lethal weapons and a cacophony of Slavic language.

"Engliski", shouted the scouts.

"Never mind the words", said Joe's man, "this isn't Dulag" or something like that in Russian. And, without ceremony they went to the nearest Russian officer. It was 1st Lt. Alec Nick Karmyzoff, infantryman from Tula (you oughta see that written in Russian!) He'd fought his way from Stalingrad — three years across Russia, Poland and Germany — to the relief of Stalag Luft 1.

Toasts are Drunk.

Karmyzoff came in the main gate. Commanding officers Zemke and Weir received him. Schnapps seared kriegie throats — glasses smashed Hitler's picture, the barracks jiggled with cheering and back-pounding. Toasts were drunk: "To the destruction of Germany — she will never rise again! And to our solid and enduring friendship." Karmyzoff went to the Russian barracks (our co-kriegies) — told them about himself, their army, and the new life that was beginning. Thus the first contact. Karmyzoff bedded down on the floor — "Rather the floor than a German bed," said he. BBC announced Hitler dead; kriegies heard the "Hit Parade" from home; the excitement was exhausting — But what an experience!

LIFE AND DEATH OF A GERMAN TOWN

TENSE MOMENTS
WHILE ALLIES
TAKE CONTROL

An air of tension hung over the camp for many days. The presence of the English and American armies on the Elbe and the Russian encirclement of Berlin made everyone feel that the end must be near. The commencement of a new Russian drive across the lower Oder toward the Baltic ports finally increased the tension to an almost unbearable pitch. Panic reigned in the Vorlager. No German had any more interest in guarding the prisoners, but only in saving his own life. Confidential reports were hurriedly burnt — and copies of "Mein Kampf" went to swell the flames.

Conference with the
Kommandant

Finally, late in the afternoon, the Senior British and American officers were called to a conference with the German camp Kommandant Colonel Warnstedt. They were told that orders had been received to move the whole camp westward. Colonel Zemke stated he was not willing to move at all, and asked in that case what the German attitude would be. The Commandant replied that he would not tolerate bloodshed in the camp; if we did not intend to move; he and his men would evacuate themselves and leave us in sole possession of the camp. When the Germans left it would be up to us to take over the camp peacefully and assume full control.

At approximately 1 A.M. on April 30 Major Steinhauer informed Group Captain Weir and Colonel Zemke that the Germans had evacuated the camp, leaving it in our charge. When the camp woke up in the morning it was to find itself no longer under armed guard and comparatively free.

Where are the Russians?

Our next problem was to establish contact with the Russian forces. It was decided to send out something in the nature of a recco patrol. An American Major, a British Officer speaking German, and an American Officer speaking Russian, set out with the German in the auto which was equipped with an American flag on one fender and a white flag on the other, to investigate the real situation in Barth and then proceed to the main Stralsund — Rostock road, some 15 kilometers south of the camp, to wait there for any signs of Russian spearheads or the proximity of the front line. The first patrol returned in the early evening. Still no sign or news of the Russian Army, but they were coming!

QUAKING BARTH
BURGHERS BOW
BEFORE REDS

As Russian tanks rumbled Northwards on the cobblestone roads from Stralsund, as Russian cavalry and guerilla troops tore hell bent for the Baltic, as the spluttering German radio flashed a staccato of place names that had gone under in the Red rip tide, Barth became an open city and an open grave. The few Americans who had been in town on camp chores from Stalag 1 knew that the life of Barth was a living death. We had seen the streets peopled by children and octogenerians, we had noticed that all males were either lame, halt, or blind; we had stared into empty shop windows, and we had seen the soldiers

LIFE AND DEATH OF A GERMAN TOWN

TENSE MOMENTS WHILE ALLIES TAKE CONTROL

An air of tension hung over the camp for many days. The presence of the English and American armies on the Elbe and the Russian encirclement of Berlin made everyone feel that the end must come. The commencement of a new Russian drive across the lower Oder toward the Baltic ports finally increased the tension to an almost unbearable pitch. Panic reigned in the Vorlager. No German had any more interest in guarding the prisoners, but only in saving his own life. Confidential reports were hurriedly burnt — and copies of "Mein Kampf" went to swell the flames.

Conference with the Kommandant

Finally, late in the afternoon, the Senior British and American officers were called to a conference with the German camp Kommandant Colonel Warnstedt. They were told that orders had been received to move the whole camp westward. Colonel Zemke stated he was not willing to make it at all, and asked in that case what the German attitude would be. The Commandant replied that he would not tolerate bloodshed in the camp; if we did not intend to move; he and his men would evacuate themselves and leave us in sole possession of the camp. When the Germans left it would be up to us to take over the camp peacefully and assume full control.

At approximately 1 A.M. on April 30 Major Steinhauer informed Group Captain Weir and Colonel Zemke that the Germans had evacuated the camp, leaving it in our charge. When the camp woke up in the morning it was to find itself no longer under armed guard and comparatively free.

Where are the Russians?

Our next problem was to establish contact with the Russians, and it was decided to send out something in the nature of a recco patrol. An American Major, a British Officer speaking German, and an American Officer speaking Russian, set out with the German in the auto which was equipped with an American flag on one fender and a white flag on the other, to investigate the real situation in Barth and then proceed to the main Stralsund — Rostock road, some 15 kilometers south of the camp, to wait there for any signs of Russian spearheads or of the proximity of the front line. The first patrol returned in the early evening. Still no sign or news of the Russian Army; but they were coming!

Russian Contact (continued from Page 1)

Every house draped with red flags (who said the Germans weren't chameleons?). Suddenly, there was Uncle Joe — — or one of his ambassadors: a chunky little Dead End guy who bobbed up and flashed a variety of lethal weapons and a cacophony of Slavic language.

"Engliski", shouted the scouts.

"Never mind the words", said Joe's man, "this isn't Dulag" or something like that in Russian. And, without ceremony they went to the nearest Russian officer. It was 1st Lt. Alec Nick Karmyzoff, infantryman from Tula (you oughta see that written in Russian!) He'd fought his way from Stalingrad — three years across Russia, Poland and Germany — to the relief of Stalag Luft I.

Toasts are Drunk.

Karmyzoff came in the main gate. Commanding Officers Zemke and Weir received him. Schnapps seared kriegie throats — glasses smashed "Hitler's picture, the barracks jiggled with cheering and back-pounding. Toasts were drunk: " To the destruction of Germany — she will never rise again! And to our solid and enduring friendship." Karmyzoff went to the Russian barracks (our co-kriegies) — told them about himself, their army and the new life that was beginning. Thus the first contact. Kamyzoff bedded down on the floor — 'Rather the floor than a German bed," said he. BBC announced Hitler dead; kriegies heard the "Hit Parade" from home; the excitement was exhausting. — But what an experience!

QUAKING BARTH BURGHERS BOW BEFORE REDS

As Russian tanks rumbled Northwards on the cobblestone roads from Stralsund, as Russian cavalry and guerilla troops tore hell bent for the Baltic, as the spluttering German radio flashed a staccato of place names that had gone under in the Red rip tide, Barth became an open city and an open grave. The few Americans who had been in town on camp chores from Stalag I knew that the life of Barth was a living death. We had seen the streets peopled by children and octogenerians, we had noticed that all males were either lame, halt, or blind; we had stared into empty shop windows, and we had seen the soldiers of the master race straggle back from the fronts dazed, whipped, harbingers of the ruin that stalked the streets of German towns. By April 30, this year of grace, the good burghers of Barth turned their faces to the wall and stopped hoping.

LET 'EM EAT CAKE

Life had not been good in the bakery shop where the camp bread was made hung a sign; cake is not sold to Jews or Poles; needless to explain that cake was not sold to the supermen either. There was no cake. But there were good things to eat in the larders of Barth, baking powder requisitioned from Holland, Nestles milk commandeered from Denmark, wines looted from the cellars of France, spaghetti and noodles hijacked from Italy, Worcestershire sauce which had trickled through mysteriously from England, olive oil drained from Greece, in short, all types of blood from the turnip of Europe. If Mussolini considered the Mediterranean his sea, Hitler considered the world his oyster and was trying to serve it up to the Reich on the half shell.

A House of Cards

As the first explosions from the flak school reverberated under the sullen Baltic sky, the new order toppled on Barth like a house of cards. Red flags and white sheets began to appear in the windows of the ginger bread houses. Flight was futile and the old stood querously on their door steps, wringing gnarled hands and weeping. Pictures of Hitler were torn down and scattered like confetti. Two German children came wailing into the bakery shop. They had heard American airmen ate little boys and mother said the day of reckoning was at hand.

Barth, like the whole of Deutschland-über-alles Germany, was on its knees in terror. But mayhem did not materialize. Wine, not blood, flowed through the streets. We got drunk.

of the master race straggle back from the fronts dazed, whipped, harbingers of the ruin that stalked the streets of German towns. By April 30, this year of grace, the good burghers of Barth turned their faces to the wall and stopped hoping.

LET 'EM EAT CAKE

Life had not been good. In the bakery shop where the camp broth was made hung a sign; cake is not sold to Jews or Poles. It failed to explain that cake was not sold to the supermen either. There was no cake. But there were good things to eat in the larders of Barth, baking powder requisitioned from Holland, Nestles milk commandeered from Denmark, wines looted from the cellars of France, spaghetti and noodles hijacked from Italy, Worcestershire sauce which had trickled through mysteriously from England; olive oil drained from Greece, in short, all types of blood from the turnip of Europe. If Mussolini considered the Mediterranean his sea, Hitler considered the world his oyster and was trying to serve it up to the Reich on the half shell.

A House of Cards

As the first explosions from the flak school reverberated under the sullen Baltic sky, the new order toppled on Barth like a house of cards. Red flags and white sheets began to appear in the windows of the ginger bread houses. Flight was futile and the old stood querously on their door steps, wringing gnarled hands and weeping. Pictures of Hitler were torn down and scattered like confetti. Two German children came wailing into the bakery shop. They had heard American airmen ate little boys and mother said the day of reckoning was at hand.

Barth, like the whole of Deutschland-überalles Germany, was on its knees in terror. But mayhem did not materialize. Wine, not blood, flowed through the streets. We got drunk.

With some 9,000 men in the camp, I am sure there were many who forfeited a D-Bar to obtain this issue of the *Barth Hard Times*, but after almost a half century, I am sure there are not many copies still in existence. I intend to keep mine.

Epilogue

They shall not grow old — their faces won't grow any older. Their jokes stay alive — those whose presence is still with you. We don't throw memories away. We cherish them and then share them.
Flight Lieutenant, Padre, Linton-on-Ouse

*T*HERE WERE 18,000 *Canadian airmen killed in World War II, and 4,272 killed while with Six Group. Documented heroes were few in actual number, but, in actuality, all who participated were heroes in their own way. If need be they were ready to lay down their lives for their country. We remember them as they were, not as they would be today.*

Membership card in
the Caterpillar Club.

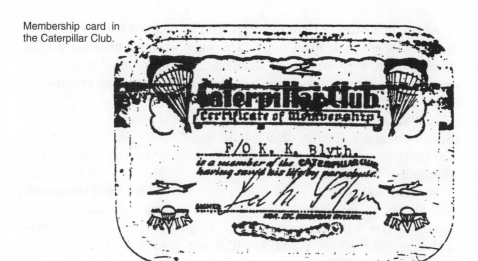

One of the unofficial decorations some members of aircrew wore after the war was a lapel pin signifying membership in the Caterpillar Club. The Irvin Parachute Company decided that because the caterpillar was the originator of the silk used in parachutes, it would be a fitting symbol to recognize those whose lives had been saved by the use of a parachute. Paratroopers did not qualify for membership in this exclusive club. It was essential that the parachute had saved one's life. If the aircraft had been out of control when one jumped, the eyes of the caterpillar were white. If the aircraft had been on fire, the eyes of the caterpillar were red. Interestingly, Irvin himself never qualified for membership in the Caterpillar Club.

Over 50 years have gone by since our experiences in World War II, yet many of these memories are as vivid today as they were when they happened. The mind can play some tricks on you — it will either let you recall the incidents in total recall, or they fade completely from your subconscious, and you have no recollection of them at all. All the incidents in this book have been told many, many times over the years, and it is quite possible they have been improved upon.

One fact is sure, if I had applied slightly more pressure on the port rudder a moment before the attack, this would have changed the alignment enough that the hit would have been direct at the tail of the aircraft. Without a tail the aircraft would have gone straight down, and no one would have escaped. For this, we all are very grateful.

Although the Cradle Crew members have all returned to civilian life, we have attempted to keep in touch. The ones who did maintain contact reached out to keep the lines of communication open. Jim Taylor was the best communicator, followed by Wat. The rest of the crew we hear from at Christmas.

In 1982, after some 37 years, we all met for a reunion in Vancouver, British Columbia. Jim, the organizer, invited Atky's wife Georgia and his son Derek to join us. You will recall, Atky had died several years earlier. We think of him often.

We have had several reunions since then. One of the most memorable was the one in Edmonton, Alberta, held at the present location of 408 Squadron, now a Helicopter Wing. The Wing had started a small museum with memorabilia from World War II. There were pictures of four Halifaxes from 408 Squadron, and one of those was *E.Q.-J* of the Cradle Crew. As we looked at the picture, the 18 *V*'s painted under the pilot's window seemed to be more prominent than they had ever been when we were at the station. Our faithful ground crew was every bit as proud of this aircraft as we were, and they had painted the *V*'s to indicate the 18 completed missions. It was because *E.Q.-J* was unserviceable that we were flying *E.Q.-Q* when we "bought it" on our 19th trip. *E.Q.-J*, along with all other Halifaxes, was dismantled after the war.

We made up T-shirts with a picture of the stork on the front, similar to what we had had on the nose of our aircraft, and on the back we had "Bargeman Johnny to Dogbark." The slogan caused a little stir and piqued the interest of 408 Squadron.

A large number of the original 408 Squadron members were in attendance, and because we had six of our crew present, a more complete crew than any of the rest attending, the squadron honored us.

In September 1993, 408 Squadron members had a reunion at Linton-on-Ouse with some 130 aircrew and their wives in attendance. In London, we attended the RAF memorial services in St. Clement Dane Church, the central church of the RAF. The floor is made of Welsh tile, and imbedded in the floor are 700 crests of the various squadrons that flew in World War II. 408 Squadron is one of them.

Nostalgia reigned when we visited the old haunts such as Benningborough Hall, Alice Hawthorne Pub, and, of course, the air station itself. Benningborough Hall, now an art museum, was the home for many of the aircrew in attendance. They recalled that at night they would walk to the

The Alice Hawthorn Pub, the hangout of the NCOs living in Benningborough Hall.

Alice Hawthorne Pub, a short distance away, only if they were able to cross a narrow part of the Ouse River to get there. The pub was built in 1865 and named after a racehorse that had 50 first- and second-place wins out of 69 races and then went to stud and produced a derby winner. The boatman fare going to the pub was always cheap, but after the guys had partaken of a few ales, the boatman would raise the fare for the return trip. There were a few instances when the boatman went home, and in order for them to get back to Benningborough Hall it was necessary for them to swim across the river with their clothes balanced precariously on top of their heads.

At Elvington station, briefing rooms have been maintained as they were then. Amazing as it may seem, although the Halifax bomber played an important part in World War II, there is only one Halifax in existence today. The staff at Elvington station has restored a Halifax with parts found in diverse locations. Two engines were located in France, and the mid-section of a wrecked Halifax was found on the Isle of Lewis, in the Outer Hebrides, off Scotland. It had been written off as scrap after a crash 40 years ago and was sold to a farmer, who was using it for a hen house. The farmer was persuaded to donate the fuselage to the museum. An RAF Chinook helicopter transported it from Lewis to the mainland, then transferred it to a truck, which brought it to Yorkshire.

A visitor to Elvington in 1986 donated a Halifax four-gun turret frame.

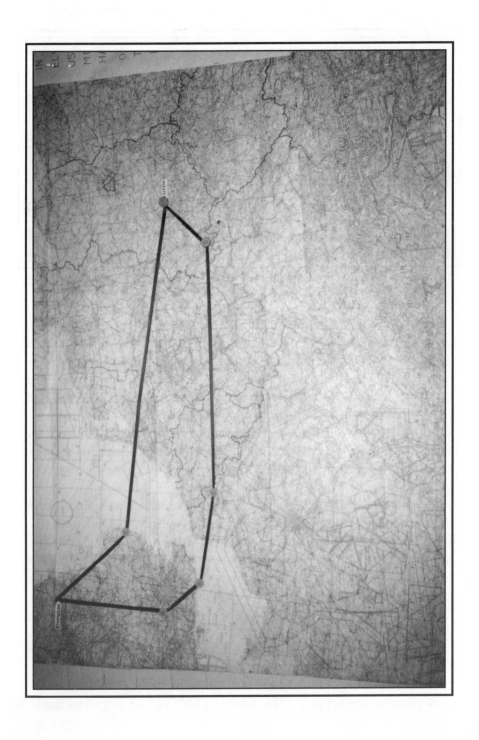

Opposite and above: Briefing-room charts.

Someone else donated a badly damaged rear turret that was restored after 1,000 hours of labor by aviation buff Bernard Jefferson. A tail wheel was recovered on the Isle of Harris, and someone donated a main under-carriage, wheels, and tires. The only major component totally rebuilt is the nose section. At one time the staff was trying to secure the nose unit on display at the British War Museum.

At Elvington, a NAAFI — Navy, Army, and Air Force Institute —

A reunion 50 years after the war: back row, Ken and Jim; front row, Doug, Brock, Wat, and Ray. Atky was deceased.

lunch room is still in operation. All aircrew personnel remember the NAAFI.

There are some additional new buildings at the squadron, but most of the old ones are still in place. The station itself is now a training location for aircrew. The trees in the open area are fully grown. The museum contains pictures of aircraft and aircrew from World War II, and our aircraft, E.Q.-J, is one of them. The mess hall remains basically unchanged after almost 50 years. Of course, this is true about all of England. If it can be maintained as it was, so it shall be.

Some time ago the Canadian Press reported that Karl Kjarsgaard, from Ottawa, Ontario, had been searching the globe since 1985 for a Halifax bomber. He found one under 750 feet of water at the bottom of Lake Mjosa in Norway. It had been there since April 1945. He was successful in raising the money needed to retrieve the aircraft and ship it to Canada as a tribute to the many Canadian aircrews that lost their lives flying these heavy-duty bombers during World War II. This particular bomber, NA-337, stationed at the Royal Air Force 664 Squadron, had flown on its last mission from England with supplies and weapons for the Norwegian underground, which was fighting the German occupation forces. After dropping their supplies, they were hit by ground flak, and they ditched in Lake Mjosa. The only survivor was the tail gunner, Thomas Weightman, still living today, who participated in the recovery project.

After the surfacing was completed, the Halifax was taken apart and shipped to the RCAF Museum in Trenton, Ontario, where it is on display. The tedious job of restoration is underway; a conservative estimate indicates it will take until the year 2000 before it is completed. That aircraft and the one at Elvington will be the only two Halifaxes in existence of the 6,200 built.

Shortly before this book went to press, the Cradle Crew was saddened by the passing of J. Brock Folkersen, May 12, 1997. He was doing what he liked best — playing golf in Yuma, Arizona — when he had a massive heart attack. Through meeting and staying in close touch, our crew has become a close family, and we are deeply grieved at the loss of our mid-upper gunner. We are grateful for the many happy times that we have shared with Brock and Vonnie over these past 52 years.

In the Foreword I have described the pilots and crews that actually attacked E.Q.-Queenie on March 31, 1945. This information was acquired through the Militargeschichtliches Forschungsamt, Abteilung Ausbildung,

Information and Fachstudien III in Potsdam, Germany. Collectively, the eight members of JG-7 who attacked us participated in over 1,244 sorties and accomplished 223 aerial victories.

I had hoped to make personal contact with Hans Grunberg, Franz Schall, or Gerhard Reiher. At this writing, however, I have not been able to learn whether any of them are still living.

Frankly, the Cradle Crew members of *E.Q.-Queenie* consider themselves very fortunate to be alive today.

Index

by Lori L. Daniel